ENDORSE

CW01506938

We all need a team that can suppoi ___ ___ ___
intercession. Charles and Liz have been longtime friends and trusted
intercessors for our work. I highly recommend Charles, Liz, and WISE
as a valuable addition to any organization that wants to ensure that
the spiritual foundation of its calling is secure.

— Os Hillman
President, Marketplace Leaders
author of *Change Agent,* "TGIF-Today God Is First," and other works

I have been researching, writing about, and leading prayer
movements for twenty-five years, and I stand amazed at the ways
that God has been moving prayer leaders into exciting new areas
of effective intercession. Outstanding among them are Charles
and Liz Robinson, who have been breaking new ground in the
area of professional level intercession. Charles's comprehensive
training manual will show you how you, yourself, might fit into this
captivating and kingdom-impacting ministry. You will be glad you
have this book, and you will be glad to have read it!

— C. Peter Wagner
Vice President, Global Spheres, Inc.
author of *Warfare Prayer, Acts of the Holy Spirit,* and other works

Dr. Charles and Elizabeth Robinson are ordained ministers under
Christian International. They have always been passionate about their
roles as ministers in the marketplace, and they have now put together
a tangible book in order to help others operate as spiritual counsel
and prayer support providers to businesses worldwide. In this
book, the Robinsons have gone deep to share wisdom to help others
minister effectively in the business world.

— Bishop Bill Hamon
Founder, Christian International Ministries Network
author of *The Eternal Church, The Day of the Saints,* and other works

I really believe in what Charles and Liz Robinson are doing, and
this book describes the how-tos of a kingdom service that can really

be of significant value for those arising on the mountains of society; it will help equip them for success.

— Johnny Enlow
author of *The Seven Mountain Prophecy* and other works

Combining proven intercessory practices of the past, Charles has added a strategic prophetic focus that will launch a new level of intercession and kingdom advancement. Those who utilize these concepts will bring intercession to a higher plane of freshness and impact. May a new generation of intercessors arise!

— Randy DeMain
President, Kingdom Revelation Ministries

Through this book Charles will teach you how to make a living at the new and exciting field of professional level intercession. Every serious intercessor should use this manual to go to the next level, which gives specific prayer strategies for use in the seven mountains and teaches how one can be compensated for this important work. I highly recommend this book.

— Dr. Bruce Cook, Founder/Convener, K.E.Y.S.
author of *Aligning with the Apostolic* and other works

LET HEAVEN INVADE
THE SEVEN MOUNTAINS·OF CULTURE

BECOME
A PROFESSIONAL
LEVEL INTERCESSOR

DR. CHARLES ROBINSON

SPIRIT-LED
PUBLISHING

LET HEAVEN INVADE THE SEVEN MOUNTAINS OF CULTURE
BECOME A PROFESSIONAL LEVEL INTERCESSOR

Copyright © 2014 by WISE Ministries International
All rights reserved. No part of this publication may be reproduced, distributed, or transmitted in any form or by any means, including photocopying, recording, or other electronic or mechanical methods, without the prior written permission of the publisher, except in the case of brief quotations embodied in critical reviews and certain other noncommercial uses permitted by copyright law. For permission requests, write to the author, addressed "Attention: Permissions," at the e-mail address below:

Dr. Charles Robinson
info@coachmybusiness.com

Special discounts are available on quantity purchases by corporations, associations, and others. Orders by US trade bookstores and wholesalers—for details, contact the author at the e-mail address above.

Scripture quotations are from THE HOLY BIBLE, NEW INTERNATIONAL VERSION®, NIV® Copyright © 1973, 1978, 1984, 2011 by Biblica, Inc.® Used by permission. All rights reserved worldwide.

Editing team: Say It Well! & Inksnatcher
Cover design team: Inksnatcher & Allison Metcalfe Design
Photo of Dr. Charles Robinson: Allison Metcalfe Photography

First Edition, 2014
ISBN: 978-0-9904902-2-7
Publisher: Spirit-Led Publishing

I dedicate this first series to my wife, Liz, with thanks for her love, wisdom, and revelation, and to my son, Nathanael, who is a sign of the type of ministry God has called us to.

I also dedicate this book to our faithful and powerfully anointed intercessors—without whom this work could not go forward—and to our future intercessors, who will blanket the world's leaders with their empowering prayers.

ACKNOWLEDGEMENTS

Special thanks to Cathy Buettner's writing services at Say It Well! for taking ownership of this project and for guiding me with grace and patience as I refined this book, on a compressed timetable. Your generosity with your Spirit-led anointing in reorganization, training, editing, and marketplace ministry transformed this work. Cathy, you are a gem!

Special gratitude to Fred and Dorinda Trick, and to all our clients and friends. Your partnerships and friendships have impacted Liz and me in ways that only God knows. This work is a testimony to the lessons learned by each of us as we have worked together.

We thank Sally Hanan of Inksnatcher, who has been a divine connection to make the final preparations on the manuscript for publishing. Your knowledge of the publishing industry and your skillsets are broad and amazing; you quickly produced excellent results. Thank you for blessing this kingdom assignment with your work.

We also thank Allison Metcalfe of Allison Metcalfe Photography and Design for how she seamlessly integrated with Inksnatcher to design and format this book's cover and interior and to insert, redo, or acquire graphics as needed to enhance the text. Her attention to detail and eye for beauty have brought these words up higher.

TABLE OF CONTENTS

FOREWORD

God is speaking to many in the church today about the role of the seven cultural mountains of influence and how strategic they are to influencing the culture for Jesus Christ. What was birthed in 1975 through Bill Bright, of Campus Crusade, and Loren Cunningham, of Youth With a Mission, is just now being realized as a core strategy to influence the culture.

We have learned that it only takes 3-5 percent of leadership operating at the top of one of these cultural spheres to actually shift the mountain—as evidenced by the gay rights movement, which has shifted the public's view of its issue by using arts & entertainment and media to reframe the public's view of it.

One of the important ingredients to this new strategy focus is the intercession required to prepare the soil for effective ministry to these seven areas. Charles Robinson has given us a new resource tool for those called to intercede in the seven cultural mountains.

The Lord tells us that is it "not by might, nor by power, but by my Spirit." Prayer must be at the forefront. Ezekiel 22:30 tells us that God is looking for someone to stand in the gap so that the land might not be destroyed. This book will help you understand God's prayer strategy to affect the seven cultural mountains.

I highly recommend this resource to help you consider becoming a mighty prayer warrior and intercessor to affect the seven cultural mountains, so that we can restore the biblical foundations of this great nation and positively affect the nations of the world.

—Os Hillman
President, Marketplace Leaders
author of *Change Agent,* "TGIF-Today God Is First," and other works

PREFACE

Five Assumptions I Make as I Write This for You

Assumption 1: You are a Christian and that means, for our discussion, that you have received Christ into your heart, consider yourself born-again, and that you have been water baptized.

Assumption 2: You have a desire to help others fulfill their God-given call through marketplace intercession.

Assumption 3: You approach this topic with an open mind and a teachable spirit. You might not be charismatic in nature or believe that speaking in tongues or the gifts of Holy Spirit are for today. This book is still for you!

We can work around our differences through grace and with a desire toward unity.* I am sure you believe in angels, that they work behind the scenes today, and that you believe in other manifestations we cannot fully explain. So it is with the power of prayer. Many aspects of the power of prayer cannot be fully explained, but there is much evidence of its influence in our lives.

Do not let a disagreement stop you from reading this material. Keep an open mind. Be flexible. God may just use you to get the next great breakthrough for one of your clients as a result of reading this book.

Assumption 4: You are willing to extend grace and to be persistent. Please extend the grace to not let my limited vocabulary and verbiage be a blockage for you. God has many ways to achieve his goals, and I am the first to realize that none of us is indispensable. He can speak through a donkey and make the very rocks cry out if he wants to! I realize that the methods I describe in this manual are unorthodox, or not what some would consider mainstream. To me, that is exactly why they work. We need new solutions to problems both old and new.

I apologize in advance if I offend you in word or theology. I have made every attempt to make this treatise approachable and as biblically sound as possible. This work is replete with scriptural references. However, I am asking you to trust me. I know what works and have seen it work.

---

* Write to me at charles@coachmybusiness.com and I will respond.

One final thing I ask of you, my beloved reader, is that if (when) I step on the tail of your favorite dogma, don't cease reading. Give me a chance to paint you the entire portrait of this new and exciting career—as I see it, and as Liz and I and our team have lived it.

Assumption 5: You will just skip forward if the marketing language in this manual turns you off. My function in WISE has been as an intercessor, sales, and marketing consultant, and as the first coach to our clients (we have since added other coaches). A portion of the book markets WISE and our associated endeavors. However, I do this because it can only help you, my reader, to receive a full impartation of the spirit of what we are accomplishing in the marketplace. As such, I recommend that you read everything in its entirety.

Keep in mind that my wife, Liz, could have written this book as well (and probably would have done a better job), but in God's providential timing, the material and ideas that I am so familiar with became this book.

Thanks,

Dr. Charles Robinson

"*Most intercession is in the religion mountain. How are leaders in the other six mountains to get the necessary intercession? Charles Robinson's company: WISE (Workplace Intercession, Support, Empowerment)*"

— Apostle C. Peter Wagner
Vice President, Global Spheres, Inc.
author of *Warfare Prayer, Acts of the Holy Spirit* and other works

"*Dr. Charles and Elizabeth Robinson have a unique perspective concerning ministry in the marketplace. Prior to their training and ordination into the ministry through Christian International, under the headship of Bishop Bill Hamon, they operated successfully in the business world and are now taking their wealth of experience to the marketplace.*

As founders and originators of WISE Ministry, the Robinsons' organization provides Christian counsel and prayer covering to numerous businesses worldwide."

— Apostle Vance D. Russell,
Founder, Arise Ministries International
author of *The Kingdom* and other works

"In the last days the mountain of the Lord's temple will be established as the highest of the mountains; it will be exalted above the hills, and all nations will stream to it" (Isaiah 2:2).

In 1975 Bill Bright, founder of Campus Crusade, and Loren Cunningham, founder of Youth With A Mission, had supper together at a conference and agreed to meet the following morning for breakfast. That night, God simultaneously gave these change agents the same dream, which they shared with each other over breakfast the following day. They saw seven mountains, which formed a larger, single mountain. God said that if they claimed the seven mountains, he would give them the large mountain, which is the kingdom of God.

Figure 1 The 7 Mountains, Source: Marketplace Leaders

The message was that if we were to impact any nation for Jesus Christ, then we would have to affect the seven spheres or mountains of society, which are the pillars of any society. These seven mountains are business, government, media, arts and entertainment, education, the family, and religion. (There are many subgroups under these main categories.) About a month later, the Lord showed Francis Schaeffer the same thing. In essence, God was telling these three change agents where the battlefield was. Here was where culture would be won or lost. Their assignment was to raise up change agents to scale the mountains and help a new generation of change agents understand the larger story.

Intercessors are change agents.

As a change agent, an intercessor has a vital role or assignment to play out in history, and he will find that his role relates closely to his inherent design and personal interests. Ahead is a chart that breaks down an intercessor's assignment. Keep in mind that this is an abridged list, and the Lord will lead you into how and when he wants you to intercede.

A business should always be about God's business, and God's priority is always about the hearts and souls of his people and their relationships with him. When business people are in line with God's heart, then the business will succeed. The closer one walks with the Lord, the easier it is to hear his heartbeat. Our prayer is for business owners, their families, and employees to learn to hear his heartbeat and know him in a deeper way. "Now faith is the substance of things hoped for, the evidence of things not seen" (Heb. 11:1 KJV). When we are in unity with him and moving in faith, all things are possible.

The Issachar Anointing

"From Issachar, men who understood the times and knew what Israel should do—200 chiefs, with all their relatives under their command" (I Chron. 12:32).

In this hour, God is again raising up anointed men and women who know how to touch heaven and bring the wisdom from above down to earth on behalf of those greatly beloved by God—his businessmen, businesswomen, and leaders in all seven mountains or spheres of society. He is raising up people with an Isaachar anointing.

An Intercessor's Assignment
The intercessor will:
discover God's vision and desire for both the intercessor and the client,
ask God for his strategy—how he wants to accomplish his vision,
report God's strategy to his overseers,
pray for provision and financial protection, and
pray for emotional, physical, spiritual, moral, relational, and leadership protection.
The intercessor:
partners with God and moves in faith to help bring God into the business,
helps the owner fulfill God's plan and vision for his or her business,
prays for the people's hearts to unite with God's heart,
partners with God and declares God's success, even when he or she does not see it.
The intercessor commits to daily:
walk in obedience to God's holy Word,
walk in purity and seek to be in unity with God, fellow brothers, and sisters in Christ,
walk in forgiveness, confession, and repentance with everyone (Ps. 51),
not allow roots of pride, bitterness, unforgiveness, or rejection to develop in his soul,
put on the whole armor of God (Eph. 6),
proclaim and exercise his authority in Jesus's name, and
proclaim God's promises in his Word for each business's employees and workplace.

Figure 2 An Intercessor's Assignment

He is calling these anointed men and women to bring God's presence, power, and revelation to leaders outside the four walls of the church and into the marketplace. These anointed men and women, as intercessors, will lead the charge in rallying around the leaders in all seven mountains or spheres. Their intercession will help surround, protect, and free the leaders from all kinds of bondages and hindrances, and release them into their respective destinies.

Empowering You for Success

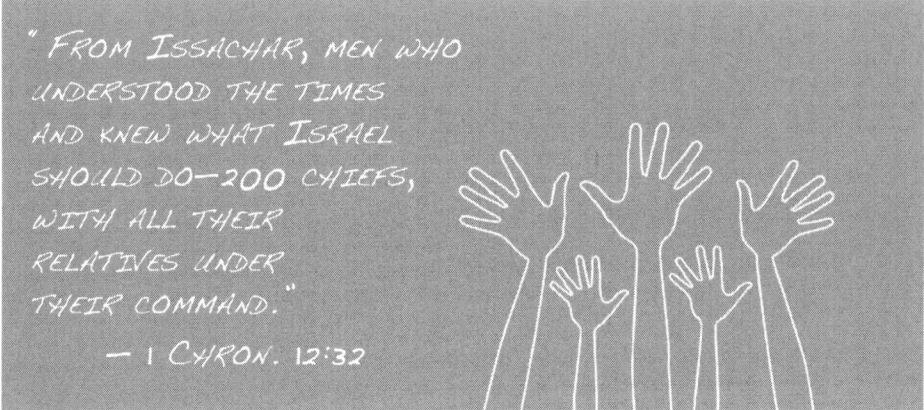

" FROM ISSACHAR, MEN WHO UNDERSTOOD THE TIMES AND KNEW WHAT ISRAEL SHOULD DO—200 CHIEFS, WITH ALL THEIR RELATIVES UNDER THEIR COMMAND."

— 1 CHRON. 12:32

The sons of Issachar would go to war for the other tribes in a heartbeat. They rose early and awakened the other tribes with the sound of the shofar.[1]

Issachar tribe members were the burden bearers of their brothers. Your prayers can wake up those sleeping clients and help them into their true purposes. As an intercessor, you are a spiritual entrepreneur, a forerunner.

God is calling these anointed men and women to bring his presence, his power, and his revelation.

As Christians, we can personally pray and apply the words from Christ's prayer "your kingdom come … on earth as it is in heaven" into our daily lives. We see an interesting corroboration of the spiritual principle in action from author John Carlson,[*] who relates a

---

* In his book, *Passion for His Presence, Entering His Gates*

message the Lord gave him about the meanings of the names of the twelve tribes. Because the twelve tribes' names are listed on the gates to New Jerusalem (in Revelation), we can assume that the presence of their names means something to our Lord, since he never wastes words in his Word. Carlson shares that because the name Issachar can indicate intercession—seen both in the words spoken at the child's birth and the blessing Jacob gave to Issachar—intercession can allow us to enter God's kingdom and to take others in with us. The gate of intercession allows us in and Jesus, himself, will intercede through us.

As Christ was to the multitudes, a multitude of priests will be to the world. This is a level of the unprecedented power and authority of Christ, himself, filling the earth with God's knowledge "as the waters cover the seas" (Hab. 2:14).

Jesus is, of course, the full embodiment of this priesthood.

Types of Intercessors

There are twelve types of intercessors based on the type of anointing they carry:

1. *List intercessor* – your personality is orderly and precise; you are faithful in completing commitments and enjoy daily covering a list in its entirety.

2. *Personal intercessor* – individuals' personal needs and one-on-one interactions motivate you.

3. *Crisis intercessor* – when you hear of accidents, tragedies, or other crises that either could happen imminently or that have already transpired, something on the inside of you rises up to take action and intervene.

4. *People group intercessor* – you feel compelled to intercede for certain cultures, or alienated or suppressed groups, to enter into their struggles.

5. *Financial intercessor* – you are a person motivated by the need to see God's provision in people's lives or situations; you have a proven ability to see breakthrough in your own and other people's finances.

6. *Governmental intercessor* – righteousness and justice motivate you;

you are a person who honors our governmental leaders.

7. *Mercy intercessor* – you are motivated by (even unwarranted) compassion for people and their needs and failings; you weep easily over people's faults, weaknesses, and infirmities.

8. *Issues intercessor* – social causes and their injustices often anger or upset you.

9. *Soul intercessor* – you are outreach oriented; God uses you to bring many to him.

10. *Worship intercessor* – you enter into the presence of God and wage warfare in the heavenlies through adoration of the Trinity.

11. *Warfare intercessor* – conflict with the enemy excites you (this anointing is strongly related to that of a worship intercessor); you like Scriptures that talk about the vengeance of God on the head of the enemy; you find the need to walk or pace rather than sit or kneel during prayer.

12. *Prophetic intercessor* – God gives you information about other people, situations, or events; you frequently receive mental pictures about people, places, or things; what you say often comes to pass.

Identify Your Intercessory Anointing

When you enter an Intercessors Certification program, one of the first things you should discover is your type(s) of anointing and how to maximize what you carry for the kingdom. The Lord usually calls a Christian with at least one prayer anointing, and often gives several different anointings. Even if we discern that we have two or three anointings, one anointing may easily seem to be our main passion or calling as an intercessor.

WISE

When God led us to form WISE, "Workplace Intercession, Support, and Empowerment," he let us know that WISE was going to empower leaders and their employees in the marketplace by helping them fulfill their callings in their businesses and other enterprises. God gave me (Charles) a corporate anointing and let me know:

- He wanted us to take his presence and power outside the four walls of the church and into the marketplace.
- He was going to use our business, entrepreneurial, management, and leadership skills to let heaven invade the seven mountains of culture.

God has since let us know that the "Issachar anointing" was going to be in operation in WISE, and that he was going to partner the religion mountain with all of the other mountains to:

- fund the end-time harvest through bringing his modern-day Josephs' wisdom and discernment to multitudes, and
- empower his people on the seven mountains for success (the inspiration for our WISE slogan: "Empowering you for success").

Our Background

At the time of this writing, we (Charles and Liz) have brought the word of the Lord to thousands of people. As experienced church and corporate pastors, intercessors, chaplains, teachers, and business owners, we and our team of intercessors and business consultants are equipped to support and empower you and your ministry for success. In 2005 we founded a dynamic local church in Austin, Texas, where we served together as senior pastors for five years.

We are now corporate pastors to many organizations, both nationally and internationally, empowering them to impact all seven mountains of influence. We are committed to, and passionate about, training and imparting the wisdom, understanding, and experience the Lord has given us. Our mission is to develop strong, mature ambassadors and warriors for Christ, and to bring the saving knowledge of Jesus Christ to our nation and the nations of his world. One of the ways we do that is through our four certification courses in a series called "Let Heaven Invade the Seven Mountains of Culture."

Course Schedule and Format Options

Certification courses happen monthly. Find them here:
- markteplaceintercessors.com,
- marketplaceceos,
- marketplacecoaches.com, and/or
- marketplacegenerals.com for prices and offering dates.

Both the group and independent study formats offered give the student impartation, wisdom, and experience from personal contact with WISE instructors.

We want to impart spiritual truth to those individuals who feel a call to the ministry of intercession and/ or coaching. We want to help leaders in all spheres (especially those in business) fulfill their divine callings from God.

Professional intercessors and coaches need to learn how to market and teach their prospective clients the value of their spiritual services and the need for the client to engage those services.

When we chose to become professional level intercessors, we experienced many pitfalls along the way, but the Lord helped us overcome them all. Ideally, in order for you to succeed in this career, you should also have some entrepreneurial and or business skills—skills in what it takes to run your own business. *Entrepreneur* magazine has some excellent material on the steps needed to start and operate any business.

If you are prepared to work hard, have some sales and technical/ computer skills, and you have a strong relationship with God, then success is imminent.

My Prayer for You!

I pray for your seven mountains intercessor, Lord, that you would bless him (or her) and give him favor in the mountains and marketplaces that you have called him to, and that you would draw leaders and open their eyes to the need for this ministry in their lives. Lord, help your intercessor to grow this ministry and launch out in faith into the deep.

God, I pray for a special impartation of the sevenfold Spirit of God, according to Isaiah 11:2-4: "The Spirit of the Lord will rest on him— the Spirit of wisdom and of understanding, the Spirit of counsel and of might, the Spirit of the knowledge and fear of the Lord—he will not judge by what he sees with his eyes, or decide by what he hears with his ears; but with righteousness he will judge the needy, with justice he will give decisions for the poor of the earth."

I pray that every God-given word in this book would be planted deep inside your intercessor and be recalled when he needs it. Lord, I pray that every ability and anointing I have would now descend upon the intercessor and that he would do greater works than me.

Lord, I pray for my intercessor's family and spouse, and for his or her leaders who need protection, who need healing, who need deliverance, who need to know that someone cares and has their backs. I pray that you would open the windows of heaven right now over the intercessor's life and ministry, in the name of Jesus, amen!

Module 1: Endnotes

1. DeMain, Randy. "God is Moving Again with Holy Fire – His Manifest Presence is Coming Upon the Priesthood." www. elijahlist.com/words/display_ word.html?ID=12660 (accessed June 18, 2014).

2. Femrite, Tommi, and Billie Boatwright. Intercession Workshop, Austin, TX, April, 2007. Table compiled by Cathy Buettner of Say It Well! Writing Services.

Recommended Additional Resources

Books

Wagner, C. Peter. *Prayer Shield: How to Intercede for Pastors, Christian* and *Leaders and Others on the Spiritual Frontlines* Prayer Warrior Series (Book 2)

Carlson, John. *Passion for His Presence, Entering His Gates*

Servello, PR Mike, *God's Shield of Protection*

Intercessors, Discover Your Prayer Power (see endnotes) gives excellent details about each of the twelve types of anointing the Lord gives to intercessors. It lists a biblical example for each type, describing the strengths and zeals each type of anointing instills in an intercessor, and even noting pitfalls for each type and suggestions on how to avoid those pitfalls. In addition, the chapter on each intercessor type ends with a short list of five or six insightful questions, which can help intercessors discern which of the twelve types of anointing they have. *Intercessors, Discover Your Prayer Power* can be helpful to you and a powerful resource for those you enlist as intercessors.

Website articles

Johnson, Nita (LaFond). "Melchizedek Priesthood." www.worldforjesus. org/articles-prophetic.php?ID=4.

Entrepreneur magazine business startup material, www.entrepreneur.com (see Startups)

DVDs/CDs

Randy DeMain's sermons on the Sons of Issachar, www. kingdomrevelation.org/product/sons-of-issachar

People

Bruce Cook, Kingdom House Publishing, Kingdom Economic Yearly Summit (KEYS), and Glory Realm Ministries
www. kingdomeconomicsummit.com

Elizabeth Alves, Increase International
www.increaseinternational.com About Us

Cathy Buettner, owner of Say It Well! Writing Services

Tommi Femrite, Gatekeepers International
www.gatekeepersintl.org

Billie Boatwright, Holy Ground International
www. holygroundinternational.org

Groups

Christian Business Network, Austin, TX | www.austincbn.org

International Christian Chamber of Commerce | www.iccc.net

PROFESSIONAL INTERCESSION

"Our company has supplied equipment to contractors for more than ten years. In 2012, sales were $883,000. In 2013, sales were $1,554,000—a 76 percent increase. Why? How could we have done it again? We could not come up with anything that we or our staff had done that was responsible for more than a few percent. We had a meeting with our staff and came to the same conclusion—all of us start every day at the office by praying together. We have given the business to God, we are his shepherds, we love to give, and we partner with WISE Ministries. Charles and Liz Robinson give us ongoing personal prophecy and counseling. Their intercessory prayer team is indefatigable, and gives us written reports every two weeks on what God is saying as they pray for us. God takes good care of his own, and he gets all the glory!"

— EH, President

2

"I looked for someone among them who would build up the wall and stand before me in the gap on behalf of the land so I would not have to destroy it, but I found no one" (Ezekiel 22:30).

As a professional level intercessor, you will function in many capacities; you'll be part of a team that applies spiritual intelligence to the work of the seven spheres of culture.

What Is Professional Level Intercession?

In this new career field called professional level intercession (named as such by apostle C. Peter Wagner), professional level intercessors (PLIs) are those trained in intercession. PLIs have a certain spiritual giftedness which allows them to see or hear in the Spirit, or both. These people usually have some secular skills, especially in business or via involvement in the seven mountains, such as video editing, teaching, business accounting, producing—any skillset or experienced background that would give them special insight or authority to pray. PLIs can be on the church staff list in the same way that retired ministers or part-time counselors are.

As a PLI, you will interface with your clients, as well as with intercessors, to create a spiritual climate in which each client can have maximum protection from the enemy.

The leader communicates with the Lord to identify the kingdom assignment(s) he has for his enterprise. You will help the client learn how to receive his assignment(s) from the Lord and communicate his message clearly to his target market. Your work will assist all your clients to follow God's model for their enterprises and for their personal daily lives, and it is wise to match your unique strengths with your clients' particular needs.

Helping Leaders Hear the Voice of God Better

WISE does not (initially) come in and tell the leader how he (or she) should run his enterprise or how to manage his employees. However, after trust is built, the consulting arm of what we do can get involved with personnel issues and strategic directional issues. We exist to help the leader better discern and know the voice of God for himself. We become a sounding board for the leaders to confirm that they really do hear the voice of the Lord—more than they may realize.

> *"My sheep listen to my voice; I know them, and they follow me"* (John 10:27).

It's a privilege for all of God's people to hear his voice, but we all can hear more clearly as we exercise this gift. As a certified intercessor, your job is to be a cheerleader for your leaders. You are there to encourage them to pursue the Lord's voice and to help build their faith. God wants to build you a platform to minister to influencers from behind the scenes.

Why Pray?

Prayer is the single most powerful force for change in the universe. E.M. Bounds, a noted prayer warrior, said,[2]

> "Prayer is the greatest of all forces, because it honors God and brings Him into active aid."

He also stated,

> "Everything depends on prayer, and yet we neglect it not only to our own spiritual hurt but also to the delay and injury of our Lord's cause upon earth. The forces of good and evil are contending for the world. Had there been persistent, universal, and continuous prayer by God's people, long ago this the earth would have been possessed for Christ."

God allows us to partner with him in prayer to change situations. Someone may ask, "God is sovereign, so why do I need to pray?" The answer is that God is sovereign, but God, in his sovereignty, restricts himself to the limits of our partnership with him in prayer.

God directs us, but we respond in prayers that bring heaven to earth.The will of God expressed through us, and the words spoken, bring to earth not only the will of God, but also *the manifestation of what we are praying about*—for us and our clients. How does intercession differ from prayer?

The Differences Between Prayer and Intercession

When you combine focused and targeted intercession (a higher form of prayer) for enterprises in all seven mountains of society, you can change any aspects or elements of society for good at their cores.

> *Prayer is the act of obedience in bringing feelings and desires—words from our hearts—to life.*
>
> *Intercession denotes the carrying of a burden that is from God's heart.*

We can pray about anything in our hearts, but to intercede means that we choose to stand in the gap for someone or something (e.g., a cause).

In intercession, we choose to become identified with that cause or individual. The intercessor carries a burden of the Lord which oftentimes is not released from him until that which he has been given to speak, and in some cases suffer, has been accomplished.[*]

Our own Holy Spirit intercedes for us in sounds that cannot be uttered:

> *"In the same way, the Spirit helps us in our weakness.*
> *We do not know what we ought to pray for, but the*
> *Spirit himself intercedes for us through wordless*
> *groans" (Rom. 8:26).*

Jesus, himself, never ceases to make intercession for us at the right hand of the Father, as Scripture states in Romans 8:34: "Who then is the one who condemns? No one. Christ Jesus who died—more than that, who was raised to life—is at the right hand of God and is also interceding for us."

Opposition to the Paid Intercessory Model

I have been a part of a CEO round table group, during which every month a member presents his or her business model, financial reports, challenges, etc. When it was my turn to present, a particular individual had a strong negative reaction due to the coupling of words "professional" and "intercessor."

---

[*] Intercessors can obviously be both men and women.

This individual said that he was going to pray for the group on a regular basis, and more or less stated that we did not need a service that paid people to do it. I respected his comment and completed my presentation, after which several people said they were interested in the service. The next month he mentioned to everyone that he was praying for us. We thanked him, but that was it—nothing more, no prayer requests, no follow up, nothing. That situation got me thinking—the level of prayer (and not even intercession) which the round table member practiced is the intercession paradigm which leaders have been used to and are conditioned to. Friend, we need to change this. I set it in my heart to respond formally with the following set of comparisons (see the table on the opposite page) to show why the current paradigm is not enough.

Our company history illustrates that professional level intercession works. Think about our track record: How could WISE be in business since 2005 in this challenging economy (and our services are not cheap) if this service did not work? Not only have we been able to remain in business, this ministry has been our main source of full-time employment since 2005. When talking with Lance Wallnau, Lance stated that "many have tried this field and have not been successful in it, but you have; congratulations!" Our success is due to our model and calling.

The Lord often encourages us by having our clients acknowledge the powerful effects of our prayers. In one case, the intercession was so much a part of the increase that the leaders of the company got together and tried to reason how this increase had actually happened. The only deduction they could make was that it was because of the prayer! Yay God! (I must be careful to not take credit where credit is really due to the Lord; he is the one responsible, while the intercessors were his vessels.)

In the client's own words:

> "Our business has just celebrated the receipt of over $100,000 for delivering four large commercial generators. We had paid for and housed these generators in our warehouse over a nine-month period. Our customer had given us a purchase order for the generators, but was then paralyzed by state bureaucrats, who insisted he could not install the generators without their permission. This dilemma was a subject for prayer for many months.

Prayer	Professional Level Intercession
I will pray for you if I remember	I will intercede for you at regular intervals
I maybe only know a general need	I will intercede for you according to knowledge of your life, family, and business(es)
I am a generalist	I am a specialist
I do not follow up with you	I follow up and ask for status updates regularly
I do not show you that I prayed	I produce a report for you on *what* I prayed
I speak to God; I do not ask him for specifics about you or your situation	I ask God what he has to say about the situation, then listen and record specifics he gives me about you and your situation
I may not pray for you for several weeks	I pray for you 2-3 times per week
I may be praying for old, answered requests. I do not followup with you to see if **the prayers were answered.**	I pray for only current, valid needs. I will follow up and will stop praying/pray for other issues when I am notified that **the prayers were answered**
You do not know what I am praying	You know *exactly* what I am praying since I write down my prayers for you
I cannot hear God speak clearly to me about you	I hear God speak to me every day about you and others, as I am gifted in this area
I pray in my spare time	I intercede in my *dedicated* time
I do not get paid for this	I get paid well and look forward to my time on your behalf
I pray for maybe 1-3 minutes for each need	I intercede for 30-60 minutes at a time
My prayers are limited to the one or two topics that you mentioned	My intercession is comprehensive; we put eight powerful prayer shields around you and your loved ones. We pray for important meetings, travel, spouse, children, other leaders, and your important business clients

Figure 5: Prayer Versus PLI Comparison Chart

This table lists characteristics of the current mindset about prayer compared to the characteristics of professional level intercession. The table illustrates how professional level intercession is at an entirely higher level than regular prayer, and carries with it the expectation of results.

Eventually we received permission to ship the generators, just before our fiscal year end, and this week the bill was paid in full! This is definitely a victory for all of us—WISE Ministries and our company."

"We are awed by the resolution of this most difficult situation."

Review: Sons of Issachar Anointing

The sons of Issachar (I Chron. 12:32) knew the times and the seasons and what Israel was to do, when Israel was to do it, and who was anointed to do it. They were people of action who had revelation: they encamped on the Eastern (sunrise) Gate, were *servants* to their brothers in the other tribes, and were not looking for their own gain.

They have spiritual intelligence and are faithful, obedient servants whom God is raising up, whom God can trust. They build others up rather than try to build up their own ministries. They have the heartbeat of God and the frequency of heaven. They love God; through obedience they are willing to fight to the death for the people to whom they are assigned.

The Client's Job

It is to *find* these anointed sons of Issachar and *engage* them, *inform* them, *release* them, and *bless* them; then watch the favor and breakthrough that happens in lives, families, and in all endeavors!

> *Jesus said "A servant is not greater than his master" (John 15:20). Our job as spiritual coaches and intercessors is not to tell our clients, the leaders in their enterprises, what to do. Your client is to partner with those who are in the Issachar tribe, who will act as a sounding board and help fine-tune your client to God's voice.*

God Needs Intercessors!

Ezekiel 22:30 says "I looked for someone among them who would build up the wall and stand before me in the gap on behalf of the land so I would not have to destroy it, but I found no one." This is an unfortunate and sad situation. God looked for someone to stand in for the land that he would not have to destroy it. He could find no one.

Godly leaders from all walks of life are exposed; the enemy has broken through the wall/hedge or, even worse, there was never any wall and God's people are being plundered by the enemy.

> *People are going to hell, profits are being squandered, companies are going out of business, marriages are breaking, and children are being taken captive at the enemy's will, all because there is no hedge. There are no intercessors!*

We and our faithful team members have dedicated our lives for the last nine years to protecting and empowering these precious ones so that the work of the enemy in their lives would cease, and that these leaders would fulfill their divine callings from God and reach a level of actualization and fulfillment they never would have known without the coaching, mentoring, and intercession WISE's team provided.

These are lifelong relationships God has sovereignly initiated. We, they, and God take what we do very seriously. God told me to make my leaders bulletproof. That is exactly what we do, through God's Holy Spirit. Leaders are taken through our novel coaching and mentoring program of inner healing and discipleship (in the seven mountains). Their businesses are empowered to be as important to God as the local churches in their regions. Their enterprises become *outposts* for the kingdom of God in those territories with angels of war assigned to them. Their land becomes the *habitation* of angels, and their enterprises become tools *in the hand* of God for their regions, as well as for the people of their regions. Salvations occur when people walk into their businesses; people are knocked down by the power of God while walking into their establishments.

Negotiations become much easier because of the presence of Holy Spirit. Favor falls and business expands effortlessly.

I remember we had one company double in size within twenty-four hours upon signing the contract; we had not even started praying! The blessing occurred because they had become *apostolically and prophetically aligned* with us.

We have paid a great price to get to where we are, to become Josephs. Remember in Ps. 105:17 "the word of the Lord tested Joseph." That great price is all worth it to birth sons and daughters in the kingdom.

In many of our companies, we experience more of the power of God than we do in our churches. I am not putting down the church. Jesus loves his bride, the church, but the warfare in the marketplace is greater than the warfare in the church, so we need more of God's power there.

Back to the passage: there is no one to stand in the gap, to make a hedge or wall—a first line of defense against the *wiles,* attacks, and deception of the devil. Eph. 6:11 tells us to take on the full armor of God to resist the devil's plans. Leaders of all types need to be taught *how* to stand.

As you, the intercessor, pray and intercede for your clients, you become the first line of defense for them. The enemy is going to have to go through *you* to get to them. (Comforting, is it not?) That is why you must be strong in the Lord, know him, and be experienced in spiritual warfare.

> *Perhaps you identify more with being a coach, but every coach needs to be an intercessor at some level, because coaches always will pray for their clients, just not for hours per day, as may be the case for intercessors. Coaches usually pray for their clients during the coaching session.*

Doors Unlocked for YOU

Many of you reading have had profound promises from the Lord. The relationship between king and prophet, if you will, can produce the things the Lord has promised you, and you can see those great and mighty prophetic words fulfilled through the relationships that are established between you and your clients.

In many cases, these are lifelong journeys that the two of you will travel on together. Can you see this? Can you believe this? If you can *see* it, you can *have* it. This career is the manifestation or the *key* to what God has been promising you all these years, and the precious fruit of these God-ordained relationships will last forever.

Convergence

When all of the life lessons, tests, wisdom gained, and cumulative experiences come together to empower you for the main assignment of your life, you reach convergence.

As a PLI, you will enter convergence, and you will empower your clients to be in convergence as well.

"Do you know that only 20 percent of leaders in the body of Christ ever enter into convergence in the work that God has called them to do? Being in convergence is the secret to getting to the top of anything." — *Dr. Lance Wallnau,* The Seven Mountain Strategy

Module 2: Endnotes

1. WISE Ministries. "Services." www.coachmybusiness.com/services- main.php

2. Bounds, E.M. *Classic Collection on Prayer.* Sydney: ReadHowYouWant, 2011.

Recommended Additional Resources for Readers/Students

Books

Hillman, Os. *The 9 To 5 Window: How Faith Can Transform the Workplace*

Cook, Bruce. *Partnering with the Prophetic: Portfolios, Protocols, Patterns & Processes*

Hamon, Bill. *Prophetic Scriptures Yet to Be Fulfilled: During the 3rd and Final Reformation*

Wagner, C. Peter. *Prayer Shield: How to Intercede for Pastors, Christian Leaders and Others on the Spiritual Frontlines* Prayer Warrior Series (Book 2)

Alves, Beth, Tommi Femrite, and Karen Kaufmann. *Intercessors - Discover Your Prayer Power.*

Freed, Sandie. *Destiny Thieves: Defeat Seducing Spirits and Achieve Your Purpose in God*

Website articles

Wallnau, Lance."How to Crack the Code that Unlocks You." www. lancelearning.biz/crack-the-code.

DVDs/CDs

Randy DeMain's sermons on the Sons of Issachar, www. kingdomrevelation.org

Lance Wallnau, "Take All 7" 4 DVD series, www.lancelearning.com

Os Hillman, Lance Wallnau, and others "7 Mountain Strategies: Keys for Cultural Influence" Audio CD Series, www.7culturalmountains.org

People

Lance Wallnau | www.lancewallnau.com

Sandie Freed | www.sandiefreed.com

CLARIFY YOUR MESSAGE

"Charles, you gave me a word that a credit was coming to me from a lawyer. Out of the blue, a lawyer contacted me two weeks later with a surprise credit that was due to my wife from over two years ago. It was enough to cover our rent that was due in days. Praise God."

— SHC, Calgary, AB

"I could have saved myself a lot of misery over the years by watching out for those who had my back. I more than ever realize the importance of certain intercessors in certain places. I understand that having the wrong people praying for you can hinder the things God wants to do in your life. Many of these things I learned the hard way, so take Charles's information to heart and save yourself a lot of distress, financial losses, as well as setbacks that could probably have been avoided by properly surrounding yourself with a strong hedge of defenses."

— Bill Smith
CEO, Now Enterprises, Inc.

3

"I have told you these things, so that in me you may have peace. In this world you will have trouble. But take heart! I have overcome the world"(John 16:33).

"The prayer of a righteous person is powerful and effective" (James 5:16b).

Going From Intercession to Intervention

This message is basic to the job of a PLI. As a PLI, you want your clients' spiritual destinies to be clear to them and to the world. Is the destiny of your client's enterprise being interfered with, distorted, or cancelled out; or is it getting through with clarity and consistency and being reinforced?

The enemy will try to confuse or distort your message, possibly through miscommunication, worldy philosophies, and/or your own misinterpretation of the Lord's voice, leading you to give a mixed message about your product or service.

As a PLI, you can help run interference on the enemy's interference, thus neutralizing his effect on your client and your client's enterprise.

Often, the spiritual intelligence we or our clients need requires that we go from plain intercession (reactive) to intervention by running interference (proactive). We do it in the same way that football offensive fullbacks and tight ends run ahead of a halfback as he carries the ball and blocks prospective tacklers out of the way.

It could also be compared to the way your defensive players run interference for your teammates, if one of them takes possession of the ball when your team is on defense. Interference can also mean the act of illegally hindering an opponent from catching a forward pass or a kick.

Your clients' intercessors are going ahead of your clients in the Spirit and blocking the enemy so your clients can move forward.

When you run interference, you stop being passive and become active in clearing the airwaves.

PLIs run interference on the enemy.

You have a message to receive from God. Your potential clients have a message to receive from you. It's simple: clear up the communication channels to enhance the message!

Interference also pertains to linguistics. If there is a lot of babbling in your client's industry, how can he stand apart? The enemy may be trying to confuse or distort his message. Is his message getting out or is there overlap and miscommunication?

Let's ensure maximum clarity on both ends and send informed, professional level intercessors and spiritual coaches into enterprises to teach leaders how to communicate their messages well.

Your client's enterprise is a tool of heaven to bring transformation to his region and sphere of influence, and it is specifically that destiny that Satan will try to block.

One main aspect of intercession is that we, as intercessors, recognize that all who are working for the advancement of God's kingdom come into spiritual opposition from God's enemy—the Devil and his minions. The enemy's goal is to oppose the truth of God, and often takes the form of distorting the truth. The enemy would like our client, or us, to have difficulty receiving the clear messages of God for our assignment or our client's.

Placing a Hedge/Prayer Shield Around Clients

As intercessors, we seek to place a hedge of protection around those for whom we pray. In Job 1:10 Satan says, "Have you not put a hedge around him and his household and everything he has? You have blessed the work of his hands, so that his flocks and herds are spread throughout the land." Satan was affected by God's hedge of protection; his reach was limited because of the hedge that was placed around Job. Satan was like a junkyard dog on a leash; he could bark and growl at Job and threaten to charge, but only when God allowed it could he touch Job. In all cases he was not allowed to kill Job. From this example, we know the principle of a spiritual hedge works. This is what we seek to establish when we pray. In fact, there are eight powerful prayer shields or hedges that we build around our clients, their families and leaders, and even their customers.

> *Marital*
> *Safety/protection*
> *Travel schedule/major meetings/presentations*
> *Sexual/moral/ethical*
> *Physical health and well-being*
> *Family*
> *Personal/financial*
> *Business/ministry*

How to Set Up Prayer Shields

When you work as a PLI, you will construct and maintain prayer shields both for you and for your clients. As the book *Intercessors - Discover Your Prayer Power* says, there are pros and cons for constructing prayer shields, and the cons are not good reasons to not set them up. As you will see us say elsewhere in this text: leaders *need* intercessors![1]

CLIENTS: Reasons to have prayer shields

Leaders *need* intercessors. Get the spiritual protection you need for breakthrough to the next level without all the attacks from the enemy. Let your intercessors do your fighting for you so you have the time and energy to hear from God on how to lead more effectively. Don't forget to pray for yourself, also. Intercessors protect you from enemy attack and/or distractions and confirm what God is telling you.

An intercessor is a person to whom you give permission to speak into your life. When she has permission to speak into your life, God will tell her intimate things about you. Don't have spiritual arrogance; you need intercessors to help you recognize your blind spots. *Choose* intercessors you know personally, so you know their strengths and weaknesses. You don't tell all your struggles to all levels of intercessors. If you travel with your ministry, it is especially important to choose intercessors in different time zones. Hold yourself accountable to your intercessors; God is not into lone rangers.

As your authority increases, so do the attacks against you (sometimes through temptations like greed, power, pride, gluttony, alcohol, sex, and drugs; other times through the release of curses against your call, foundational teachings, fruit, marriage, health, and seed) to get your focus off what you're called to do.

If you have a business and/or ministry, you need a shield for them, as well as a personal shield for yourself. The shield size increases as the number of your employees increases.[2]

Knowing who you are in Christ—knowing your identity—unlocks your destiny.

Reasons some people do NOT have intercessors:
- They are rough, tough loners who say they don't need them. (These people are leaving themselves, their families, and finances open to attack.)
- They are uninformed and don't know about the need.
- They think they don't need prayer if they go to church; however, the reverse is true—if they go to church, they are on Satan's hit list and need prayer!
- They know they need prayer but are naïve about how important being covered with intercessory prayer is. If they don't understand the need, then they don't understand the importance of their callings.

How do you develop your prayer shield?
List people you know or think are praying for you now. Then ask. Most people are willing to surround you in prayer.

An intercessor should:
1. Be an honorable person, a person of integrity whose yes is yes and no is no, who means what she says and says what she means, who is the same person in all areas of her life, lives by the word of God, and carries Jesus Christ with her wherever she goes.

2. Be able to keep confidentiality, a person who doesn't even share a prayer request with another for the purpose of that person joining him in prayer. If your intercessor violates your confidentiality, write him a letter thanking him for serving you, but releasing him from your intercessor list. Also confront him personally about the specific issue of confidentiality you know has been violated (as per Matthew 18).
3. Be able to listen to God (she is quiet and knows how to hear his voice).
4. Understand authority and walk in it. He is confident, knows how to stand in the authority his anointing gives him, and prays boldly.
5. Be teachable and trainable. She goes to meetings where people teach about intercession; she doesn't think she knows it all, even if she is equipped.
6. Be committed to pray for you (when God speaks to him to pray for you, he knows when to pray and when to respond.)
7. Have a call from God to pray for you/your ministry/your business. God spoke to her heart to have an anointing to pray for you as an individual.
8. Be humble (agree with what God says about him, "I am an intercessor; my anointing is; God speaks to me).
9. Be willing to stand firmly in the gap for you.
10. Be able to share with you in a way that is not intimidating, and present information she has heard from God in a palatable way.

Signs that you need intercessors, more intercessors, or need to strengthen your shield

Sometimes you don't need more intercessors, you may just be missing intercessors in a certain area of anointing. See the signs:

Your ministry does not grow.

You are battle weary, worn out, and it's an effort to get up and get to your ministry.

When you see a breakthrough, you keep hitting a wall.

You find that you are beating yourself up a lot (which means the enemy is beating you up through a gap in your shield).

You begin to question or doubt God's call for you and your

purpose in life.

Your family is under attack or you get sick.

Your intercessors are under attack. (Encourage all your intercessors to have their own intercessors, and form a multilayered shield around yourself.)

You experience much backlash or retaliation. (Tommi and Bobbie, two of the authors of *Intercessors - Discover Your Prayer Power,* suggest praying for leaders for three weeks after they host any major event.)

Reasons the intercession process can be ineffective:

- Intercessors say they don't get enough input.
- Intercessors say the person they are praying for doesn't trust them. (If you can't share your heart with your most trustworthy intercessors, the problem is with you, not them.)
- Lack of feedback; be courteous enough to tell them when an answer comes—that builds their faith and encourages them.
- Lack of openness

Testimonials

"The intercession we have received from WISE for the past three years has been, and continues to be, invaluable. In the spiritual we have seen the unknown become known and understood, the hidden revealed, and the tide turned. In the natural we have seen real results, coming into a place of greater understanding about how to move forward in business. We have had a time of slower sales of our new homes, and the prayer and business intercession and timely word and insight has provided a real boost in not just sales, but in our attitude, outlook, and understanding about the future and how to walk into it. I believe that any business will benefit from the prayer and intercession services that WISE provides."

— Fred T., Tuscaloosa, AL

"We were going through a difficult time with a business partner. As I was struggling with how to handle an e-mail reply to him, I was praying when your e-mail immediately came in with the audio file. I didn't realize you had captured the prophetic ministry at the Os Hillman Change Agent conference. Thank you for sending it. I listened to it intently. God is speaking directly to me through you all. I sensed the Holy Spirit's presence there, and when I listened to it again, it affected me the same way again.

You all have a special anointing that is flowing through you and the work you are doing; one that is much needed in the marketplace. I've seen how much it's needed here, in Europe, in Asia, and all over the world. God bless you all and keep up the good work! It's important."

— Allan K., Louisville, KY

"I became acquainted with WISE at a point in my work life and life in general when I felt very stuck. I sensed I had a calling for business and the arts, and had visions that the Lord had given me regarding these. I knew that I was capable, but no matter how hard I tried, nothing I attempted seemed to gain traction or bear much fruit. I didn't understand what was hindering me; it was painful, and it was causing financial problems as well as a sense of shame, confusion, failure, and isolation.

Over the course of three months—as I participated with WISE in weekly coaching sessions, received prayer ministry, and committed myself to the process—I experienced phenomenal breakthroughs that probably would have taken several more years to happen, and who knows if I would have received all of them.

The Spirit of God was so present in our calls and in the prayer ministry, and was with us every step of the way. I know now that I am indeed a creative person who has a very real calling for business. I now have focus in direction, and the revelation of the Father's love for me is a personal reality. I am developing incredible connections and relationships in the area of the arts and business, and the blessings and freedom have overflowed to my family as well.

The level of my WISE coaching and intercession team's discernment to see beyond my blind spots, to encourage me, to speak truth, to stand with me, andto fight for me in the Spirit was a gift from God; I'm so grateful to them for that. Thank you, WISE!"

— Christina P., Denver, CO

Taking Credit

One of the weaknesses and temptations of intercessors is to take credit for what was done through our prayers. For example, we break a spirit of rebellion off of the land, city, or business, and immediate results are identified—whether in the newspaper headlines, in the boardroom, or through an order coming in. *Wow, what I prayed for was answered to a tee!*

Do we immediately claim the credit for this?

The temptation is to do so, but be careful: many others have gone before us, and many others may be praying alongside but are hidden. Taking credit for results sometimes seems dishonest to some people, and if things make a quick reversal (which can happen), it makes the claim look cheap and self- promoting. My advice is to be careful and avoid the trap of taking credit. Alwaystake the humble route.

Be especially aware of this if a group was praying together and they all prayed something different. Perhaps the answered prayer was not just the result of one person who was "right" (although I guarantee that everyone will think his bit of revelation was the true source of the answer). It may be that it was due to everybody coming together and God blessed their unity, saying, "All right, angels, do it for them!"

As an example, Liz and I were attending a spiritual advisory board meeting for one of our clients, and we were coming against the slowdown in contracts to a tune of about $150,000, which was urgently needed. I saw (in my mind) a python spirit at the door, which was holding up the blessing, so I rebuked it. Liz saw an angel in a bank-like vault that needed to be released. Another person did some deliverance on the CEO for a spirit of lack. Another said that the CEO was not being specific enough in his own prayers, so the CEO prayed specifically at that time. Finally, another person dealt with issues on the land and repentance. That very day $90,000 of the money was released!

I guarantee you that every person thought he did it and that God used him. (Wouldn't you?) This is okay, but don't blurt it out to the others and take credit. (This was not done, by the way. Maybe all of the prayers and warfare and repentance brought the breakthrough. The joy was that the team did it!)

If prompted to do so, tell people what you did, and the results, but say that you are not going to take the credit and leave it at that. People will respect that. Yours may have been the last prayer that finally pushed the thing over, but there may have been hundreds of thousands of collective hours of prayer that went into that effort.

Module 3: Endnotes

1. Alves, Beth, Tommi Femrite, and Karen Kaufmann. *Intercessors - Discover Your Prayer Power*. Ventura: Regal, 2000. [Much on the topic of prayers shields is covered in this book. The book instructs how to gather and recruit intercessors for prayer shields, how to determine which intercessor types to use in different prayer shields, and what characteristics qualify/disqualify intercessors. In addition, it gives recommendations for how to set up a regular schedule of communications, how to regularly evaluate your shields, and how or why to release an intercessor.]

2. Cook, Dr. Bruce. "Spiritual Due Diligence™" kingdomadventures.com. www.kingdomventures.com/pdf/SpiritualDueDiligence.pdf

3. Wagner, C. Peter. *Prayer Shield: How to Intercede for Pastors, Christian Leaders and Others on the Spiritual Frontlines* Prayer Warrior series (Book 2). Ventura: Regal, 1994.

Sources and Recommended Added Resources for Readers/Students

Books

Hillman, Os. *The 9 to 5 Window: How Faith Can Transform the Workplace*

Cook, Dr. Bruce. *Aligning With The Apostolic, Volume 1: Apostles And The Apostolic Movement In The Seven Mountains Of Culture*

Hamon, Bill. *The Day of the Saints: Equipping Believers for Their Revolutionary Role in Ministry*

People

Tony Stolzfus, Leadership Metaformation | www.meta-formation.com

Groups

Christian Business Network, Austin, TX | www.cbnaustin.org

THE JOSEPH CONNECTIONS

"As the founder and CEO of a company that reaches directly into all seven mountains of culture, including nearly half of all Fortune 100 corporations, our partnership with WISE Ministries has been invaluable. We would not be as effective, nor have the influence that we do, without its support and friendship."

— Randy S., Washington State

"Charles and Liz Robinson of WISE have the knowledge, the heart, and the experience to provide intercessors for business. Because of our excellent experiences as their clients, I hope the Robinsons continue to disciple many more intercessors. We know firsthand how gifted the Robinsons are, since, from 2005, we have both watched them shepherd their employees, and benefited from their guidance for us as we steered our business through many adventures.

Simply said, Charles and Liz Robinson were given to us by God, who knew that we needed the friendship, mentoring, and spiritual authority they possess to move forward in his purposes—not only in our business life but also in our personal walks with him. They are the real deal, and operate in the true anointing of Father because of the level of intimacy they each keep with him. They are our friends, comrades-in-arms in spiritual warfare, and our spiritual mentors all in one!"

— Reverend Dorinda Trick
counselor

4

"And see if I will not throw open the floodgates of heaven and pour out so much blessing that there will not be room enough to store it" (Malachi 3:10).

The Joseph Experience

God is raising up many leaders in the field of marketplace ministry through "Joseph" experiences. Os Hillman has written much about this phenomenon, in which the Lord takes a Christian in business through a difficult time of testing. The Christian businessperson may lose most or all material possessions and/or relationships in the process of refining her total dependence on God.

In the process, the "Joseph" Christians may also go through several tests to see if their character is mature enough for the leadership positions the Lord is preparing them to have in the coming revival.

Why is the marketplace such a critical area for ministry? Rich Marshall, author of *God@Work* and *God@Work2*,[1] feels the Scripture has been fulfilled in the Bible verse Luke 10:2:

"The harvest is plentiful, but the workers are few. Ask the Lord of the harvest, therefore, to send out workers into his harvest field."

Rich relates how, in the United States as well as other countries, more workers are not Christian than are Christian. However, Christians from many different denominations (the workers) are spread throughout the workforce among the unbelievers (the harvest fields). Those workers have learned how to work together in their jobs; implementing them to work together for kingdom purposes is just the next step we need to accomplish for the sake of revival.

Cities of Gold

While going through a SOZO inner healing session,* Holy Spirit told me that he wanted to take me to meet someone. He led me to a sea of hot coals. I could see Jesus in the distance. Jesus said I was to walk across the hot coals and to take my shoes off before walking. I said, "I cannot, Lord, it will burn me!" Jesus assured me that I could do it. I took my shoes off and walked across.

Next, I came upon a river of fire. Jesus was very close now, but there was no way I could go through that river. Jesus knew this was too much for me, so he stood up on his throne and reached out. (His arms became extremely long; he lifted me up over the river of fire and plopped me right on his lap!) Jesus then showed me a dark city. He threw a handful of gold and the city lit up with an amazing show of light, color, and splendor. Then he repeated the same action over another city, then another. He spoke to me and said, "Charles, I have called you as a Joseph to the sheep nations and cities." The vision ceased.

I had to go through the river of fire to reach that point. "They strengthened the disciples in these cities and encouraged the disciples to remain faithful. Paul and Barnabas told them, 'We must suffer a lot to enter the kingdom of God'" (Acts 14:22 GWT).

Josephs — Together Forming a Patchwork

Several months after the cities of gold experience, I was sitting in my office when I "saw" myself at an ironing board. I was ironing a nondescript fragment of cloth that was incomplete by itself; it had a definite color (green) and a definite texture. It was thick, appearing to be made of a heavenly substance I could not identify. It was almost as if the piece of cloth were my own life and I was processing it ... ironing out the wrinkles. I was feeling alone, feeling I was not making much of an impact. The vision expanded:

I saw many other Josephs ironing out the fabric of their destinies, ironing out the wrinkles in their lives and relationships, seemingly feeling alone and in obscurity. Next, I saw a most amazing mantle, a garment, if you will. Each piece of fabric was now sewn into each of the other pieces. Even though there were numerous colors and

---

* SOZO is the Greek word translated "saved, healed, delivered." Sozo ministry is a unique inner healing and deliverance ministry aimed to get to the root of things hindering your personal connection with the Father, Son, and Holy Spirit.

countless types of fabrics and textures, each piece fit together into the garment perfectly.

These individual pieces were not symmetrical, but all shapes and sizes, yet, when they were fitted together, not one piece overlapped the boundaries of another and there was not one gap in the garment. It was splendid! There was no lack; everything had been provided for by God and his Josephs—solutions, inventions, creativity, provision, protection—and the mantle covered it all! I discovered that this, the fabric of our lives, was Joseph's coat of many colors which will be worn by all of the Josephs, universally, in this final hour.

I subsequently did some research on Joseph's coat and learned that one reference[2] said it was a patchwork quilt. This became the theme of our Tipping Point Unconference in 2013—the coat and a new anointing for that patchwork quilt. The patchwork quilt is what God is birthing through us—his Josephs and the intercessors who support the Josephs. (Note that the intercessors who support the Josephs shall themselves also become Josephs.) The patchwork quilt provides all that is needed. There is a new wisdom and a new anointing for the times in which we live.

Daniel 12:3 states that in the latter days

> *"Those who are wise will shine like the brightness of the heavens, and those who lead many to righteousness, like the stars for ever and ever."*

You are called to shine in this new career field which you have chosen. Many will come to the Lord's light.

This wisdom is called the Daniel or Joseph anointing. We as PLIs are called to turn many to righteousness—God's righteousness and character and integrity. He will shine through us in the midst of a very great darkness (see Is. 61), and we will reflect his glory as the moon reflects the light of the sun at night. In the way that Joseph had the answers when Pharaoh asked him for the interpretation of his dream,[†] we will have the answers, the interpretations, when the questions are asked. The problems which will face us are of an

---

† Of the seven fat cows and the seven skinny cows that ate the fat cows (see Gen. 37-50)

order of magnitude greater than any problems that have faced us previously.

Spiritual Gates

We will also have the *solutions*—great and ingenious ones. We will have heavenly solutions which will have come down through us. The number of solutions and inventions will have greater impact than those which came before.

Angels reserved from the foundation of the world, who have never been released, will be released. We will operate as a modern-day Jacob's ladder which stretches to heaven—one upon which the angels ascend and descend. Most importantly, the Lord is at the top of the ladder directing the angelic activity (even over your life).

> Jacob ... had a dream in which he saw a stairway resting on the earth, with its top reaching to heaven, and the angels of God were ascending and descending on it. There above it stood the Lord ... When Jacob awoke from his sleep, he thought, "Surely the Lord is in this place, and I was not aware of it." He was afraid and said, "How awesome is this place! This is none other than the house of God; this is the gate of heaven" (Gen. 28:10-17).

Jacob named that place Bethel, which means "house of God." He redefined the purpose of that place.

Warfare to Open and Close Gates

God uses intercessors to open portals (or gates, if you will) and to displace forces of darkness over enterprises, cities, regions, and territories. Gates are very strategic. The enemy understands this as well. Warfare is ongoing in the seven mountains, more heavily in some mountains than in others. Ruling spirits fight to open and close gates of access. Opening a gate allows unhampered heavenly access to an area, while closing a gate restricts access by malevolent spirits.

An important detail to recall about gates is that the city gates were where financial transactions occurred in the city. The arts & entertainment mountain is an area where we definitely see warfare at the present time. New Age leaders understand the importance of gates in their respective regions and areas of influence, but through prayer, intercessors can specifically address and counteract the New Age takeover of Hollywood.

Gates in the Bible

Psalm 24:7-9 is all about gates:

"Lift up your heads, you gates; be lifted up, you ancient doors, that the King of glory may come in. Who is this King of glory? The Lord strong and mighty, the Lord mighty in battle. Lift up your heads, you gates; lift them up, you ancient doors, that the King of glory may come in."

As an intercessor, you are a gate opener and a territory definer.

Warfare can be at the level of principalities; remember that both fallen angels and God's angels are considered principalities. God has his principalities, his archangels. Your client's enterprise can have strong, even arch-, angels assigned to it. It also can have evil principalities operating through it because of iniquity in, or curses on, the people in those organizations, regions, or territories. We are to open heavenly portals (open heaven) of revelation over our organizations so that the angels have access when needed and so they can bring the resources "down the ladder" from heaven. By the way, you are the ladder they descend through!

In Matthew 18:16 Jesus says for every fact to be confirmed by two or three witnesses: "But if they will not listen, take one or two others along, so that 'every matter may be established by the testimony of two or three witnesses.'" I Cor. 14:3 tells us that prophecy is given for edification, exhortation, and comfort.

"But the one who prophesies speaks to people for their strengthening, encouraging and comfort."

"It is the Spirit of prophecy who bears testimony to Jesus" (Rev. 19:10b), so prophecy is the voice of Jesus. The Spirit of prophecy builds up, encourages, confirms, and brings comfort and rousing calls to change. In contrast, someone who is operating in the office of the prophet may say words that are not so comforting to people, such as words of correction, which are for their good: "And He gave some as apostles, and some as prophets, and some as evangelists, and some as pastors and teachers, for the equipping of the saints for the work of service, to the building up of the body of Christ … but *speaking the truth in love,* we are to grow up in all aspects into Him who is the head, even Christ" (Eph. 4:11-12,15 NASB, emphasis mine). The office of the prophet is the office of one operating in a much higher level of anointing of prophecy and revelation than is seen in someone who has a prophetic mantle or someone who is operating in the simple gift of prophecy.

> *As an intercessor, you are a gate opener and a territory definer.*

The purpose of this book is not to delve into the depths of the theology of the prophetic, but rather to emphasize that this gift is essential for ministering to your clients, and it is used to discern the real battle going on in their lives and in their enterprises. It is advantageous for the PLI to flow in the realm of prophecy. There are many good books on the prophetic. I recommend Dr. Bill Hamon's excellent book *Prophets and Personal Prophecy: God's Prophetic Voice Today,* and Bruce Cook's *Partnering With the Prophetic.*[3]

A New Finishing Anointing—Josephs Work Together

We are running in a finishing *new anointing* now. You see, Joseph was a planner—not just a dreamer, not just an interpreter. He was strategic and methodical. He personally supervised the building of the storage containers so that when the famine struck, *the grain was ready* to fulfill the needs of the people. That supply lasted for seven years (see Gen. 41). God is doing the same thing today and many lives shall be saved, even unbelievers', through God's *new Josephs,* of which you are a part. You must be, for how can you interpret the mysteries and the dreams of your clients and bring them into breakthrough unless you have a new Joseph anointing? This is also combined with the Issachar anointing.

> *Favor and breakthrough — you can have them in your own life and in the lives of your clients.*

Favor

If there were any areas where I could say specifically that WISE has an anointing or ability, it would be in the areas of favor and breakthrough. I would define *favor* as seeing doors open without the client having to do anything in the natural realm to cause them to open. For example, rather than favor simply showing up in the form of phone calls for orders on a new product—a product we had just advertised on the *Home Shopping Network*—favor would be the president of HSN saying, "Not only do we like the one product, but we want to add your *entire* line to our upcoming shows!" Now *that* is favor.

God's favor comes out of the blue and hits you like a ton of bricks, in a good way. God's favor floors you and leaves you speechless. God's favor does not come from nothing—you either have the fruit of favor in your life (which is produced from obedience and sacrifice)‡, or you partner with someone who has paid the price and voilà, things change almost immediately.

For example, when someone brings WISE (and you too!) on board, logjams in the spirit realm become dislodged. I can't tell how many people have said that as soon as we began to pray for them, they felt something shift. Something does shift; it's like God takes the favor which is on our lives and our enterprise and places it on our clients. Not only that, but he loves to do it! Do I sound excited about the subject of favor, God's divine favor, heaven's favor? It's because *I am*.

We at WISE have paid the price for this, although I will not go into all the reasons why. You have this book in your hands, and you will benefit from this favor as well. May it be imparted to you through the reading of this manual. We are nothing special in ourselves, but he calls us special and beloved. He is the only one who is begotten of the Father and worthy of all praise, because Jesus paid the price so that we could walk in the Father's favor.

Breakthrough

Breakthrough is a spiritual force, and it may even be an angel. Breakthrough is that supernatural power that overcomes an obstacle. It is very closely tied to the gift of faith—not just saving faith, but supernatural faith which can do the miraculous (see I Cor:12).

---

‡ the gifts from Holy Spirit, of which prophecy is but one.

Breakthrough comes in many different forms, but some of the more common ways are through praise and worship. Ascending to such a level in warfare, praise breaks through the enemy's hold over your mind, body, emotions, etc.; or someone else's mind, body, or emotions.

Breakthrough may come into a situation or circumstance by bringing a divine healing, a sudden order that was needed, or an unexpected payment. Whatever the area of breakthrough needed, angels are certainly involved as well. Perhaps the angel Gabriel is involved in delivering an important piece of communication you have been waiting for, or the angel Michael is involved in defeating the enemy that has been oppressing you, or a client (or perhaps a lesser angel) is involved in the breakthrough. *How* God does it is immaterial, but the fact that *he does it* is the point. The fact that one minute ago *something happened* and I, or my situation, or my client's situation is *not the same anymore,* means that a miracle happened. This is what WISE Ministries brings to the table. *Things change* when we come aboard; we feel the warfare immediately and go into battle, many times against a ruling spirit that is involved, and God breaks it.

God's favor floors you and leaves you speechless.

We are not novices; we have been involved in many battles with territorial spirits, spirits the Bible calls rulers in high places. "For our struggle is not against flesh and blood, but against the rulers, against the authorities, against the powers of this dark world and against the spiritual forces of evil in the heavenly realms" (Eph. 6:12). Many times the battle is totally invisible and does not manifest in the natural; however, sometimes it manifests in the natural with signs and wonders.

Expect breakthrough as a trained intercessor. Your clients desperately need breakthrough, although they most likely could not put it into words. Breakthrough comes through Holy Spirit administrating or directing the angels on the behalf of another through you, your words, and your body.

You are a conduit for his flowing power and administration. Your words are eternal and powerful and divinely inspired as you direct the flow of the river of God to bring that needed breakthrough to the earth realm from the heavenly realm.

Experience his love and his breakthrough and his favor right now. Enjoy it, bask in it. You are going to a new level right now; by faith claim it and receive it. Receive a new anointing!

Module 4: Endnotes

1. Marshall, Rich. *God@Work* and *God @ Work: Developing Ministers in the Marketplace*, Vol. 2. Shippensburg: Destiny Image Publishers, 2005.

2. Myers, Erin. "Patchwork Quilting — A History Summary" Fibre2Fashion. www.fibre2fashion.com/industry-article/ business- management-articles-reports/patchwork-quilting-a-history-summary/ patchwork-quilting-a-history-summary1.asp

3. Hamon, Bill, and Oral Roberts. *Prophets and Personal Prophecy: God's Prophetic Voice Today.* Shippensburg: Destiny Image, 2011. Cook, Dr. Bruce. *Partnering With The Prophetic: Portfolios, Protocols, Patterns & Processes.* Lakebay: Kingdom House Publishing, 2011.

Recommended Additional Resources for Readers/Students

Books

Hillman, Os. *The 9-5 Window: How Faith Can Transform the Workplace*

DVDs/CDs/MP3s

Hillman, Os. "How We Lost the 7 Mountains" MP3, www.tgifbookstore.com

People

Rich Marshall, ROI | godisworking.com

C. Peter Wagner, Wagner Leadership Institute www.wagnerleadership.org

CHARGING FOR PRAYER

"I have been using the services of WISE Ministries for the last three months and have found it to be a tremendous blessing. The team has been very supportive of me, and my coach was great. She always had an encouraging word to say and many words of wisdom.

The prayers and support I received really helped me, and I know that the Lord was answering those prayers and healing me of various issues and challenges I was facing. It was great to know that I had a team of committed people supporting me through some very difficult times.

I wouldn't hesitate to recommend WISE to anyone."

— Natalie B., Darby, England

5

"Now to the one who works, wages are not credited as a gift but as an obligation" (Romans 4:4).

"The worker deserves his wages" (Luke 10:7b).

You Are Paid to Solve Problems

The ultimate breakthroughs all belong to God. We move in his power, his revelation, and his grace. Jesus said "I no longer call you servants, because a servant does not know his master's business. Instead, I have called you friends, for everything that I learned from my Father I have made known to you" (John 15:5). God will make you look good. Remember that. You look good when you simply follow his advice and are obedient in relating and, in some cases interpreting, revelation.

Obedience is the currency of heaven. Jesus said, "If you love me, keep my commands" (John 14:15). Obedience is equivalent to love in the Bible. If you are obedient, you will be successful in solving problems for your clients. Solving problems entails getting to the root of those problems. There are many different types of problems which need solving—financial, marital, personnel, operational—or controlling spirits, confusion in the marketing and message, etc. Sometimes the problems have to do with the leadership and those who have hired you. As I said before, your allegiance must be to the Lord, who is your ultimate employer. He will help you to urge and coax your clients, in love, to change.

> "Therefore, I urge you, brothers and sisters, in view of God's mercy, to offer your bodies as a living sacrifice, holy and pleasing to God—this is your true and proper worship. Do not conform to the pattern of this world, but be transformed by the renewing of your mind. Then you will be able to test and approve what God's will is—his good, pleasing and perfect will" (Rom. 12:1-2).

He has called your clients to their lines of work. "Being confident of this, that he who began a good work in you will carry it on to completion until the day of Christ Jesus" (Phil. 1:6).

You Charge for Prayer? New Times Demand New Methods

I need to rephrase the question. You charge for the intercessor's time? The answer is YES. The prayer is offered up freely, but the time is not. In other words, the time of the intercessor is valuable and, as such, he should be compensated for the time spent in lifting up the client's needs.

One major purpose of this book is to validate and verify that the need in the intercession field is both for professionalism and for accountability.

Say you are a pastor. Do you charge your congregation for each sermon that you preach? That would be absurd. Your congregation supports you for your time and the value of your ministry. So think of your clients as your supporters in the ministry to which God has called you and for which he has gifted you; your clients are paying for your time.

We don't pay our pastors just to preach a sermon; their ministry is much more expansive than that, and so is the ministry of the PLI. It's so much more than prayer; it's spiritual discernment, confirmation, encouragement, recording (via reports) what God is saying. It's warfare against the spiritual forces that are coming against you and your enterprise, devising strategies to defend against and prevent spiritual attacks, going ahead of the enemy in the Spirit.

Too long have we relegated spiritual ministry to being free and not dared charge for it. My well thought-out and rehearsed answer to questions goes like this:

"You pay professional pastors, you pay professional missionaries, so why not pay professional level intercessors? Are they not as important to God as pastors?"

Wait; come to think of it, don't ask that! The truth is intercessors are just as important, and so is the machinist, the janitor, and the CEO too! Our work is our ministry, period. We don't differ in importance to God, just in our function. The word "work" in Greek, the language of the New Testament, comes from the root word "avodah," which is the same root word as for the Greek word for worship. We worship in church, and we worship in work and *through* our work.

Too long have we in the church thought of intercessors as consisting of only a group of ladies who have their mornings free, and who have met together for years on Thursdays. Our churches have not honored these ladies as intercessors, recognized or acknowledged which anointing(s) they had, trained them to further develop their gift of intercession, or had excitement about recruiting others—both men and women from all age groups and different segments of society—to join the prayer teams.

Intercession in the local church has appeared weak at best and a social club at worst. "Remembering you in prayer" may have meant only that your name is uttered on a list, one of hundreds on Thursday mornings, if the person reading names at that time didn't fall asleep! (Sorry, that wasn't nice.) So I am writing this to bring these intercessors into the twenty-first century ministry and to combine their gifting in business, art, education, or government along with the spiritual gifts.

Intercessors Are Like the Hidden Treasure

"For Scripture says, 'Do not muzzle an ox while it is treading out the grain,' and 'The worker deserves his wages'" (I Tim. 5:18).

"We always thank God for all of you and continually mention you in our prayers" (I Thess. 1:2).

"And the people came to Moses and said, 'We have sinned, for we have spoken against the Lord and against you. Pray to the Lord, that he take away the serpents from us.' So Moses prayed for the people" (Num. 21:7 ESV).

"The kingdom of heaven is like treasure hidden in a field. When a man found it, he hid it again, and then in his joy went and sold all he had and bought that field" (Matt. 13:44).

When your clients find you, they will do anything for you because you, as the intercessor, are the key to their breakthrough. You have been hidden just for your client. God has already given you the land.

Therefore, do not let your giftedness remain buried any longer. You are a treasure hidden in darkness. "I will give you hidden treasures, riches stored in secret places, so that you may know that I am the Lord, the God of Israel, who summons you by name" (Isa. 45:3). Only when you are found can your light shine forth. "Arise, shine, for your light has come, and the glory of the Lord rises upon you" (Isa. 60:1).

Money Is Spiritual

We are discussing the topic of finances for two very important reasons. First, *you* have to be good with your finances—good with God (not under condemnation), as well as good with the concept of being paid for your services and that you are worth what you charge. Second, spiritual services are worth being paid for.

God loves a cheerful (hilarious) giver: "Each of you should give what you have decided in your heart to give, not reluctantly or under compulsion, for God loves a cheerful giver" (II Cor. 9:7). Whatever we do, we need to "work at it with all your [our] heart, as working for the Lord, not for human masters" (Col. 3:23). We give to man in the frame of acting as a channel to God.

God's Promise of Prosperity

"Most people do not see prosperity in their lives because they do not expect to prosper! … What we expect from life is often a direct result of our desires, whether they are Holy Spirit-prompted or not … This is a time to break out of the shell of your last identity, whether good or bad. God is doing a new thing with his people and creating a new model of kingdom authority in the earth. You are a part of this! It is time to break the spirit of poverty from your life. Poverty thinking is contrary to faith, and without faith you cannot please God. You please God when you have a mind to prosper."

— Chuck D. Pierce & Robert Heidler[1]

Prosperity is not just financial success. Prosperity has within it the meaning of success at all levels in life: physical, emotional, mental, spiritual, etc. I am prosperous if I am doing the will of God and if there is peace in my marriage and family. As PLIs, our job is to seek prosperity the way God has defined it, for ourselves and for our clients.

Why Should a CEO Compensate You for This Ministry?

Robert says that the tithe belongs to the Levite (pastor), and that special offerings such as firstfruits belong to the priest (the

> "Give the first and the best to sanctify the whole and the rest."
>
> — Robert Henderson, *The Caused Blessing*

apostle). Otherwise, how can the apostle function (without finances)? If apostles go unfunded, it will lead to a diminishing of the apostolic work in the earth. When we are properly aligned with the apostles, the church and all spheres of society will see great breakthrough. This is why WISE has adopted this model. Support is needed for this new function in the seven mountains.

- This is part of the reward for the coaches and intercessors, and it is given into the apostolic ministry. The apostolic ministry has the ability to fully reproduce its DNA. Scripture says that there are different levels of rewards or multiplication— some thirty, sixty, and hundredfold (see Matthew 13:23). The soil is important, and it is what produces the increase. The apostolic soil is the most productive. Not all ministries produce the same fruit, and God is calling on us to examine those ministries and to listen to God's voice as to where to give. Coaches and intercessors are *good ground.*

- Remember, apostles bring breakthrough. Apostolic ministry has the ability to remove

> "Modern-day Levites are pastors and modern-day priests are apostles."
>
> — Robert Henderson, *The Caused Blessing*

mountains and to bring favor too, because it is largely assisted by the angelic realm and carries with it the authority of heaven (to make decrees). The apostolic ministry is preceded by meekness— power under control. Moses was a type of apostle, and he was the meekest man on the face of the earth (see Numbers 12:3).

- This is an ongoing relationship; the client is not paying for an answer or a breakthrough, but is supporting a relationship. Again, relationships are paramount. God wants to support you, but you must have wisdom. Desire the best for your clients and love them, protect them, and pastor them;. Then they will want to provide for you because the two of you are in covenant—many times for life.

- PLIs are on a par with church-paid ministerial staff.

The purpose of this book is to update and inform intercessors that there is a professional and certified level of intercessory expertise and involvement you can provide within all seven mountains of culture. Trained intercessors can even operate in the local church in order to bless it. The main point here is about honor and expertise in making things happen for your clients through God in you.

This is a level of proficiency that deserves financial compensation and recognition similar to that for other church staff positions. For too long the intercessors have been in the prayer closet. Now God is calling you into the light, and to—as the apostle Paul said to Timothy his son—"discharge all the duties of your ministry" (II Tim. 4:5).

Money is spiritual.

> *"For where your treasure is, there your heart will be also."* (Matt. 6:21)

God wants to intervene in your clients' lives, he wants to solve their problems, and you have the ability to serve them. The essence of what we do in intercession is that we come alongside and show our clients that they are not alone. We do life together as family. Even if they do something wrong, as long as their desire is to please the Lord, God loves them and does not judge them; he can get them back on the right path. You (and your clients) will decree a thing and it will happen. "Surely then you will find delight in the Almighty and will lift up your face to God. You will pray to him, and he will hear you, and you will fulfill your vows. What you decide on will be done, and light will shine on your ways" (Job 22:26-28).

Intercessors are like Peter out fishing for a breakthrough, answer, or direction from God. Peter was a professional fisherman and fished with nets, but when Jesus sent him to find a fish so he could pay his taxes, Peter used a hook. The hook speaks of accuracy and specificity—the kind of prophetic guidance our clients need. One fish and one hook; let's connect ... God has a problem in a person's life with your name on it. The problem is being used to get that person's attention so that he can connect with you to get him to where he needs to be. God allows the problems in people's lives for a reason. Your client may not have a business problem, but rather a marriage problem that God wants to work on. God has a hook in his sons and daughters, and he needs to work on a specific issue; that is why the client is seeking you out. In another sense, the client is the fish with the coin in his mouth—the coin that solves your problem too.

We all have problems or needs and God is keenly aware of them. Every coach needs a coach and every intercessor needs an intercessor. These relationships are always a win-win. Be prepared to be challenged and enriched by your clients. They are not necessarily paying you for an answer—they are paying you for your relationship with God (your ability to hear, your wisdom, your discernment, etc.). You can teach someone to fish or you can provide him with the fish. Jesus told Peter to cast his net on the other side of the boat. We need God's techniques and new strategies for this hour.

We establish a baseline and a benchmark that recognizes and rewards those trained.

Remember, you are in the relationship business and you are there to solve problems. The larger the problems you solve and the more influence you have, the more you will get paid. This is the law of increasing returns. Here is the law of risk and reward: the greater the risk you take, the more you will be rewarded. As an example of risk in this line of work:

God is waiting to bless your clients. What is needed is for you to walk into their lives. You are like a key to a door that has been locked. God just places the key (you) in the lock and turns it to open the door. Sometimes the door is stuck shut and some WD-40 needs to be applied (think of this as the anointing and release from spiritual warfare), but the door will open eventually.

Why Do We Charge for Intercessory Services?

Here at WISE, we have, in the past and also currently, given free services to many clients for many months ... our reason being that we feel the Lord is telling us to do so, and/or we want potential clients to see the value of our services, and/or are aware that some cannot afford to pay for services at the time, yet they really need ministry, etc. Why not always give it away? That is the question many have in their minds. It originates with people being confused about the value of spiritual ministry and the separation of church and business. Which mountain supports spiritual ministry: the church or business?

We, as good church members, have focused on giving to God with our tithes and not on funding the pastoral staff or the church mortgage. This has been good for church leadership, but not so good for us.

We don't associate that 5 percent of our tithe just went toward the preaching of a sermon or toward having the lights on on Sunday morning. There has been a lack of specificity regarding *where* our money goes. For example, when I was young I gave thousands of dollars to a well-publicized ministry. Did my money go for winning souls or for a fountain in the new building? *I don't know.* Our giving as Christians can sometimes seem to go into a black hole.

As a result, good church people are used to giving to God, but not to paying for specific, spiritually oriented services. Counseling is the exception, but serving others with your gifts and anointing is about relationship and honor. How do you place a price tag on honor? This is the challenge.

There needs to be a *knowing* that you and your client have been placed together by God for mutual benefit, and that your client needs you in order to reach his or her destiny in God—not just in business, relationships, or finances, but in his *destiny*. Issachar speaks to this; tribe members honored and cared for their brothers and sisters in the other tribes. They lived to see the other tribes become successful and would fight anyone who stood in the way. Your clients need you to recognize and awaken their potential and calling in God.

Honor

WISE exists to be an extension of the church for our businesspeople. Businesspeople are used to being the ones who write the checks and solve the problems in a church. Is the extent of their ministry ushering, or receiving the offering? Quite frankly, they are used to being prostituted; many pastors see their businesspeople as being provision for their own visions. Businesspeople are not generally honored in the church. Our number one goal as intercessors and coaches is to honor and encourage our people.

Module 5: Endnotes

1. Pierce, Chuck D. and Robert Heidler. *A Time to Prosper, Finding and Entering God's Realm of Blessings.* Ventura: Regal, 2013.

Recommended Additional Resources

Books

C. Peter Wagner, *Prayer Shield: How to Intercede for Pastors, Christian Leaders and Others on the Spiritual Frontlines* (Prayer Warrior Series)

Robert Henderson, *The Caused Blessing: Connecting to Apostolic Power Through Strategic Giving*

Bruce Cook, *Aligning With The Apostolic, Volume 3: Apostles And The Apostolic Movement In The Seven Mountains Of Culture*

Bill Hamon, *Prophetic Scriptures Yet to Be Fulfilled: During the 3rd and Final Reformation*

DVDs/CDs

Randy DeMain's sermons on the Sons of Issachar, www. kingdomrevelation.org

People

Robert Henderson, Robert Henderson Ministries www.roberthenderson. org

Randy Demain, Kingdom Revelation Ministries www. kingdomrevelation.org

Bill Hamon, Christian International Ministries Network www. christianinternational.com

ESSENTIAL TOOLS

"Pastor Charles prayed prophetically over my wife and me in February 2009. Among many personal words of the Lord that were received and clarified throughout the year, there was a word given about our investment business, Kingdom Legacy Fund. The Lord spoke through Charles and indicated the fund would have returns of over 100 percent, and even up to 800 percent coming. I must admit, my mind didn't really grasp those levels of returns as our best year was 18 percent, and the worst ever was just over 12 percent; we considered those to be good enough for anyone.

As I prepared for strategic planning for 2010 by just doing some number crunching, I calculated that we had increased capital to invest by 846 percent, and the annual return for 2009 was 100 percent better than our best year—18 percent in 2002 to 36 percent in 2009. The numbers didn't translate in my mind as earnings, but they did translate into impact for our company and for our clients. We are grateful to WISE for its continued prayer for our business, clients, and principals of Kingdom Legacy Fund."

— John M., Fort Lauderdale, FL

6

"Not by might nor by power, but by my Spirit, says the Lord Almighty" (Zechariah 4:6b).

Praying for Leaders and Their Unique Needs

Leaders have unique responsibilities and pressures that you need to understand as a PLI, and you won't understand them unless you have been a leader and run an enterprise (such as a business). Things happen. Leaders have to stay on top of every obstacle that comes their way—meet payroll during difficult times or shortfalls, deal with an IRS audit, cover the loss of two leaders who give their notices at the same time, attend to a lawsuit, all within the space of a few days … need I say more? As a new PLI, ask the Lord for a Romans 12:15 "rejoice with those who rejoice and weep with those who weep" baptism and identification with your client. Until you identify with him (or her) and his leaders, the Lord may not give you glimpses into his heart and into his struggles. That type of insight is essential before you can weep between the porch and the altar, as a modern-day priest, for your clients.

> *"Let the priests, who minister before the Lord, weep between the portico and the altar. Let them say, 'Spare your people, Lord. Do not make your inheritance an object of scorn, a byword among the nations. Why should they say among the peoples, "Where is their God?"'"* (Joel 2:17).

You need to ask the Lord if you are called to each potential client. If so, *then* the Lord will give you his burden for him and his needs. Make sure your clients are giving you regular updates on their needs, and that they either communicate them to you in person—on the phone/Skype or via e-mail—at least every two weeks, but preferably weekly. It is easy for them to lose track of their changing needs and the need for them to communicate these to you, so I encourage you to remind them often, especially initially. As the pain of change becomes greater than the pain of staying the same, they will be prompt in connecting with you.

A Typical Intercession Session

As a PLI, you can expect your typical prayer session to go like this:

You read the latest e-mail updates from your client.

You put on some worship music.

You pray in the Spirit (if you have your prayer language).

You pray specifically.

God may speak some prophetic utterances or give you a mental picture and its interpretation. God will speak to you in the ways and manner in which you are gifted. Be open for *new* forms of communication from him. God will help you and give you insight.

Frequency

We ask that our intercessors pray for the time recommended per week. You set your own schedule, but make sure it is not just all on one day. This keeps the coverage smoothed out.

> *"Surely the Sovereign Lord does nothing without revealing his plan to his servants the prophets"*
> (Amos 3:7).

Clients who are seeking intercession for their enterprises may have many questions they want answered.

How can I know that my business or enterprise has the favor of God? Can we receive the results that we would like?

Will doors be opened to new business without us having to do it via our own efforts?

Can families of leaders be at peace? Can employees be at peace with each other?

Will financial doors be opened?

Will God still prosper us in the midst of attacks—whether verbal, gossip, slander…?

Is the enemy resisting us, yet unable to stop us? Is our faith being tested?

Does God care about my enterprise? Can God be involved with my enterprise above and beyond just blessing it in some general amorphous sense?

What hidden dangers exist if I am passive in my Christian walk toward my enterprise?

What if there are hindrances that I am unaware of? Can my enterprise be healed and set free from these hindrances?

I feel like I am walking the tightrope right now. What can I do?

What part do I play in the success or failure of the enterprise as its leader? How can my enterprise be a powerful tool in the hands of the Lord in its own right?

I am not sure that I can continue if things do not change. Is there help?

The answer is YES! You can help in the way we have helped hundreds of others. There is hope!

> *"We are 'birthers' for God. The Holy Spirit wants to 'bring forth' through us. Jesus said in John 7 : 38, 'From his innermost being shall flow rivers of living water.' 'Innermost being' is the word koilia, which means 'womb'. We are the womb of God upon the earth. We are not the source of life, but we are carriers of the source of life. We do not generate life, but we release, through prayer, Him who does."*
> — Dutch Sheets, *Intercessory Prayer*

The Importance of Revelation

God knows our future! God knows your client's future. Being able to hear God's voice is paramount in this new industry.

I cannot overly stress the importance of being able to hear God's voice *for yourself;* this is an ability that all of God's children need to have. (In John 10: 27 Jesus said, "My sheep listen to my voice; I know them, and they follow me.") I also cannot over stress how important it is for you to cultivate the ability to hear the voice of God *for others* when in this line of work.

There are gifts of Holy Spirit[†] outlined in I Cor. 12 and I Cor. 14 which mention the revelatory functions of Holy Spirit, such as the word of knowledge, word of wisdom, and discerning of spirits. These gifts, combined with the gift of prophecy (which we are actually told to covet in I Cor. 14:39 KJV, and to "desire earnestly the best gifts" (I Cor. 12:31 KJV) of which prophecy is at the forefront), creates a prophetic flow. This prophetic flow is divinely powerful in providing revelation and confirmation, and in answering questions.[*]

Specifically, prophetic flow gives revelation about:

- what's-next type of questions [real time prophetic (RTP)]
  » "What is God going to do?"
- global, overall, general company direction
  » "What should we do?" and
- God's in-depth knowledge about our lives and situations.

Prophetic flow reminds us that God cares about our businesses and our livelihoods and wants to *invade* our enterprises (but he will invade our enterprises only with our permission, since Holy Spirit is a gentleman).

Interceding in this way is very closely related to the real time prophetic ministry (RTP). Intercession and RTP work together. You cannot have one without the other, and when used together, the quick revelation as to what is wrong or what is needed, followed by the apostolic decrees and prayers to get the job done, are priceless to your client.

Can you see how powerful this is? RTP enables us to be in direct communication with God and to enable quick answers, strategies, and solutions. Remember that when you are interceding, there is a difference between knowing what the problem is, knowing what to rebuke in certain situations, and then in commanding the breakthrough. This is a three-step process, not just a "God, answer my prayer" process.

A final thought for this section—notice we don't just ask God to

---

[*] Before I continue on this subject, I'd like to clarify my terminology for Holy Spirit: I do not refer to him as The Holy Spirit. I don't call myself "The Charles"; I say simply my name, Charles. Holy Spirit is his name, he is not a thing, a "the" or an "it"; he is the most powerful spirit in the entire universe, a spirit whose name is Holy.

bring the breakthrough. He says, "You do it."

We command the breakthrough.

"Bind their kings with fetters, their nobles with shackles of iron, to carry out the sentence written against them—this is the glory of all his faithful people" (Ps. 149:8-9). As PLIs, God has given that authority to us—"the glory of all his faithful people." We are the enforcers of heaven's decrees and you, as a PLI, are the one who unlocks the mysteries of unanswered prayer. Unanswered prayer and enigmas are solved, logjams are released by prophetic/apostolic intercession, and solutions are implemented by those in authority, all at your word. Sounds like an important job, wouldn't you say? Do you think there is more of a need for the PLI ministry in our increasingly complex and interrelated world?

The Importance of the Baptism in Holy Spirit

For completeness, I need to mention that being baptized into Holy Spirit, with the evidence of receiving a prayer language (tongues), is essential. In fact, Holy Spirit gives the aforementioned gifts as the fruit of receiving the baptism. I will not delve into all of the scriptural references to this here, but know that the baptism is the *gateway into the supernatural spiritual realm* in which the PLI operates. Without Holy Spirit, you will be unaware of spiritual forces, both good and evil, which are in operation in your clients' lives (and in your own life). Without him, it will be impossible to get to the root of the spiritual problems for which you are interceding. The baptism allows you to discern the true battle.

The gifts allow you to exercise authority over evil and are your weapons of warfare (see II Cor. 10:4).

The weapons we fight with are not the weapons of the world. On the contrary, they have divine power to demolish strongholds. Without being skilled in the use of these weapons of warfare, do not even contemplate entering this line of work.

God will train you in spiritual warfare. It is a free gift.

Scriptures Referring to Holy Spirit

If needed right now, after reading the following Scriptures, ask God to fill you with Holy Spirit.

> *Do not get drunk on wine, which leads to debauchery. Instead, be filled with the Spirit* (Eph. 5:18).
>
> *These people are not drunk, as you suppose. It's only nine in the morning! No, this is what was spoken by the prophet Joel: "'In the last days, God says, I will pour out my Spirit on all people.*
>
> *Your sons and daughters will prophesy, your young men will see visions, your old men will dream dreams. Even on my servants, both men and women, I will pour out my Spirit in those days, "I am going to send you what my Father has promised; but stay in the city until you have been clothed with power from on high"* (Luke 24:49).
>
> *"But you will receive power when the Holy Spirit comes on you"* (Acts 1:8).

The type of apostolic or prophetic intercessory ministry, which is the essence of a PLI's job, is filled with various tests at various levels in the kingdom down through the years of your training, before you arrive at the level God has called you to walk in. It's kind of like God's version of the holodeck on Star Trek, which was used for training purposes and diversion, although this was real.

Know that God will be with you in these moments. My advice to you, having done all in these situations, is to just stand. "Therefore put on the full armor of God, so that when the day of evil comes, you may be able to stand your ground, and after you have done everything, to stand" (Eph. 6:13).

What Is a Destiny Link?

We are all born with innate spiritual strengths and weaknesses. We come into this world needing each other. We grow in life needing each other, and this need for each other can be called *destiny links.*[†] Types of destiny links include:

someone sent by God to get you to your next assignment, or

a seasoned advisor who has already been where you are going, e.g., Jonathan and David, Elijah and Elisha, Paul and Barnabas

---

† a term coined by Sandie Freed in *Destiny Thieves*

Each Enterprise Is a Spiritual Entity and Has a Destiny

An enterprise, whether profit or nonprofit, is a spiritual entity. It has a spiritual destiny to fulfill (from God). As God's sons and daughters, we are creators, like our Father. I believe that every organization needs to give a percentage off the top to worthy causes. This and other attributes are ascribed to *kingdom companies*.

> *Organizations provide provision and sustenance for the owners and employees, but they also have a social responsibility to their regions and are to be giving centers.*

When God places a creative spark inside a company's founder, it is because he has a *life* purpose for the company to fulfill—a spiritual blueprint which encapsulates its destiny. This destiny may be unfolding; it may not be known in its entirety early on.

When God saved and called your client, he put a destiny and a blueprint inside him with detailed instructions on what he has called him to do on the earth. One of these outworks is your client's enterprise(s). (I don't just call it a business, because we could be talking about a studio, political office, family, classroom, TV or radio station, or church, etc. Each one of these examples is a part of God's— now man's—creation, and is a part of the kingdom of God if it has been properly dedicated and commissioned by God.)

In the 2013 Tipping Point Annual Unconference, we awarded our Social Transformation Company of the Year Award to the Atlanta, Georgia-based CKS Packaging.[‡] CKS gave 2.8 million dollars from their top line to over forty-eight ministries in 2012. They feed and clothe and help prepare children for school by distributing backpacks and supplies to literally thousands of children and adults through their Maximum Impact Love ministry,[§] which is on company grounds. They directly impact the neighborhoods in which they work.

‡ www.ckspackaging.com
§ www.ckspackaging.com/our-company/social-responsibility/maximum-impact-love/

God Is Not a Slacker

Is it not amazing that your leader (and you) and I arrived on this portion of the earth in this time to do this particular thing? God is so much more grandiose, and his processes so much more complete and lengthy, than that which we have even imagined. God is not in a hurry; he takes his sweet time! I just turned fifty as I write this, and as I look back at half of a century, I realize that God works much more completely, yet much more slowly, than I was led to believe when I was first saved. I can see how his second coming may not happen quite as quickly as I and others have thought and taught. That is not to say we should be slack.

> *"The Lord is not slack concerning his promise, as some men count slackness; but is longsuffering to us-ward, not willing that any should perish, but that all should come to repentance" (II Pet. 3:9 KJV).*

Intercessory Tools

Listed below are just a few of the intercessory tools you might use as a PLI; we find the ones we have listed here to be helpful.[1] Please note that this text and book are designed for use by intercessors with varied backgrounds and experience. When we include a list such as this, we assume that you will seek out a trained intercessor if you see a tool with which you are not familiar, or about which you would like to learn more. You can also contact WISE (see back of book for contact information), and we will help guide you to our master offerings, or to a training source we recommend for that tool or technique.

Listen to God, seek his heart on the matter, ask for his strategy/ plan, and then pray.

Decree
Worship
Write
Anoint
Prayer-walk
Bind

Fear God in truth
Hear and declare
Claim his promises

A prayer: *Lord, help us all to discern the signs of the times, but also to be diligent—with the gifts and connections you have given to each of us and in the fulfillment of our callings.*

Chapter 6: Endnotes

1. Intercessory Tools taught by Elizabeth Alves and team leaders. "Intercessory Training." Intercessors International, 2005.

Recommended Additional Resources for Readers and Students

Books

Cook, Dr. Bruce. *Aligning With The Apostolic: Apostles And The Apostolic Movement In The Seven Mountains Of Culture* (Vol. 1-5)

Hamon, Bill. *The Day of the Saints: Equipping Believers for Their Revolutionary Role in Ministry*

Freed, Sandie. *Destiny Thieves*

Sheets, Dutch. *History Makers: Your Prayers Have The Power To Heal The Past And Shape The Future*

Goll, Jim. *The Lost Art of Intercession: Restoring the Power and Passion of the Watch of the Lord*

DVDs/CDs

Pierce, Chuck, Robert Heidler, Linda Heidler, Paul Wilbur and Chris Hayward, "Positioned for Advancement: Understanding the Tribes and Months." www.gloryofzion.org/webstore

Os Hillman, "Reclaiming the 7 Mountains of Culture Introduction."

www.tgifbookstore.com

People

Chuck Pierce, Glory of Zion International
www.gloryofzion.org

Anthony Hulsebus, Dominion Ministries
www.dominionministries.net

Bishop Bill Hamon, Christian International
www.ChristianInternational.com

Groups

Christian Business Network
www.christianbusinessnetwork.org

Elizabeth Alves, Intercessors International
www.increaseinternational.com

Preparing Well

"I've only been with WISE for three months, but already see benefits. Prayers that I'd been praying for quite some time have been answered on the fast track. God is doing the work, but I believe he is pleased when his children partner together to come before him. I also appreciate WISE's interest in my family, as family issues can affect business. WISE's weekly counsel has been inspiring and thought provoking. If you're unsure as to whether to partner with WISE for prayer and support ... go ahead and take the risk...God honors our faith."

— Anonymous

7

"You will also decree a thing, and it will be established for you; and light will shine on your ways" (Job 22:28 NASB).

What Is Strategic Intelligence?

Before I discuss strategic intelligence, I want to talk about spiritual intelligence. We have heard of other intelligences, such as emotional intelligence. Spiritual intelligence, which is also very appropriate, is the ability to ask and to know which spiritual forces and/or dynamics are in operation.

Is the source good or evil?

Is this a demon spirit, an angel, Holy Spirit, or a human spirit?

Spiritual intelligence also helps one know how to react and respond in a variety of situations, especially in professional situations. Know your audience. Being consistently involved at the board level is one of the highest honors in our business.

Strategic intelligence, for our purposes, carries with it all the ideas above, but it additionally has a *strategy* or *stratagems* for both the enterprises and for each individual product, service, or project the enterprises are engaged with.

Signs of the Need for Spiritual Intelligence

Your potential clients may be considering intercession because they feel as if something is lacking, but they cannot quite identify what is missing. Some possible explanations are:

They have tried everything else and still find themselves lacking.

They wonder why some of their prayers, or the prayers of their intercessors, haven't been answered.

They have achieved a level of success in their enterprises, but wonder why they haven't gone to the next level.

They wonder why it seems as if they are caught up in the world's way of doing things and can't break free.

They lack a detailed roadmap of where God wants to take them and their ventures.

No one has been running interference for them and deflecting the attacks of the enemy.

No one has given them the spiritual intelligence they need.

They don't have a team that can listen to the chatter through advanced spiritual intelligence, such as the sample story in II Kings 6:8: "Now the king of Aram was at war with Israel. After conferring with his officers, he said, 'I will set up my camp in such and such a place.'"

They don't have a ministry team which immerses itself into the DNA of the client and company, one that seeks the Lord in order to understand the times and the seasons of the enterprise's impact through its products and services.

Enterprise — as Important to the Kingdom as the Church

God is "into" networks, and as such, your clients' business(es), ministry, studio, governmental office, school, etc. can become a part of the regional, national, and international network of heaven. The fact that your client's enterprise resides on land and in buildings is hugely important. It is all about the land. Land and buildings have occupants at many levels, and both have a spiritual memory. We must take this into account when dealing with issues related to cleansing, as well as to armaments and fortification that the Lord desires to bring into a region or territory.

God wants to use your client's property as a beachhead to minister to your region! He wants to use it as a regional apostolic hub.

There is authority in financing and in manufacturing, and in ministering in any way that your client can minister to people. What a powerful tool is your client's enterprise in the hand of God!

If the leadership is teachable and pliable, there is nothing God cannot do through the physical aspects of your client's company—it becomes a natural extension of heaven's spiritual effects. Again, it's all about the land. Every establishment can be an armament for the kingdom and part of the heavenly network—a launching point, which is just as important as the local church (but which differs in function) for God's angels to the territory and the region. Does this not excite you? It excites me! Put another way, God wants to use your clients' lands and buildings for his purposes.

Spiritual Blueprint

Strategic intelligence enables you to create a plan for success in the competitive marketplace of your company in the areas of advertising, sales, new initiatives, etc. Whether or not your involvement reaches into these areas is up to the leadership and its trust in you.

Battle Plan

A plan that the spiritual coach or intercessor will have some involvement with is a battle plan. This is a strategic plan that addresses the issues and resistance, both within and without (outside) the company, and will be an additional bonus for your client.

The battle plan is a strategic intelligence plan that addresses all resistance, territorial spirits, competitors, and issues that have to be overcome. The battle plan is a forward-looking document that consists of strategies and tactics in advancing the kingdom of God through the outworking of the enterprise.

Strategic intelligence has to do with how to respond to the plethora of spiritual, management, tactical, personnel, financial, and operational issues which can arise. Remember, every issue that the company faces has a spiritual component to it. Strategic intelligence has to do with what is really going on, not just the superficial symptoms, and how to respond to it. Again, this means getting to the root of things. Consider a doctor in the act of diagnosis. As he methodically examines the patient and takes note of the symptoms, he is able to reach a conclusion that may not be initially obvious to the layperson. The doctor arrives at his deductions using a number of diagnostic tools. Similarly, the spiritual advisor uses a number of spiritual diagnostic tools.

Why Do Spiritual Warfare?[1]

It's all about the people—souls.

To expose the darkness against a client and his enterprise and allow for the illumination of Holy Spirit

To pray for a client's needs in order to help him become more productive

To bring unity to a family, workplace, and/or situation

To help him know God and his presence and develop a greater relationship with him

To help him grow in faith and knowledge (of God's Word)

Spiritual Warfare Expectations

As you embark on your journey as a PLI, you will undoubtedly experience new and even intense kinds of spiritual warfare. Do not be afraid. This is the first rule of intercession. Know that as you cover others, God will cover you.

I often see spiritual gold given to me as a result of enduring an attack. Sometimes, for example, if we have an issue with pride, we may get attacked—not only because the enemy has found a legal right to do so, but because the attack may lead us to repentance. It could indeed humble us. In the middle of our attack, we can recognize our sin, repent and ask for justice, because Jesus paid our punishment.

Therefore, the results of the sin which led to the attack can be turned around within twenty-four hours when we repent.

When we hear what the enemy is saying, we know the issue we need to deal with. The point is to get ourselves as pure and clean as the Lord so that we have no "real estate" in us which the enemy can claim as belonging to him.

Jesus said the enemy was coming and had nothing in him. Nothing in Christ belonged to Satan, and nothing Satan could claim as his own. The object is to have everything in us look like Jesus so that all "territory" belongs to and reflects him. It really is a win-win situation.

Many say that Satan is attacking them. If so, you have to ask them if he has any legal right to do so. God is God over the Devil, and he uses him to help us become more like Jesus. "In all things God works for the good of those who love him, who have been called according to his purpose" (Rom. 8:28).

Repentance Defined

Simply saying "I repent" is not always true repentance.

Please understand, you must know in your heart that your sin has offended and hurt God.

Sit in that a moment and feel God's hurt, and be sincere in your heart's desire to change. This is important. If your son or daughter hurt your best friend, you would want to say, "I am really sorry for what my daughter or son did." It is the same situation when we ask for forgiveness—the Lord has feelings also, which we need to release. Saying you repent without really thinking about it much would be as ineffective as someone saying he's sorry in an inauthentic way—you can tell he does not mean it or feel even a drop of real remorse.

Christians Attacking Christians

Oftentimes people who are anointed by God get attacked. If they are anointed and someone starts to speak lies about them, then they can go to court. The key is to repent for that sin even if they are not guilty. Repenting shuts the enemy's mouth. What then can the devil say when you say "I repent," and do not even try to defend yourself? Jesus does that, his Word does it, and he is the Word. When you follow his example, then the accusation becomes the thing that is judged.

Many very anointed people do not malign others, because people have died after being judged for their accusations. If you say anything negative about another believer, that believer immediately begins to feel the effects of your negative comments because you just gave the enemy the legal right to attack them. Christians can give footing for the enemy to attack ministers because of lies spoken about them by fellow Christians. The maligned ministers can go to the court of heaven on that issue and stop the attack.

A spirit of accusation has been released against the body by the body in this hour, e.g. by the *Strange Fire* book.[2] We cannot throw the proverbial baby out with the bathwater just because of some (and I admit rather egregious) errors in the body of Christ. There are over 500 million Spirit-baptized believers in the world, and the Charismatic and Pentecostal believers are the fastest growing segment of Christianity. Why? Because Holy Spirit gives us our weapons of warfare through the gifts of Holy Spirit (outlined in I Corinthians 12 and 14). Without the gifts we are not even aware of the battle, let alone able to fight it.

Get Ready to Be a PLI

Get trained, but don't do this until God tells you that you are ready; stepping out too early could leave you open to spiritual attack. [Be sure to say connected to, and covered by, an intercessory group, church, or mentor, because your alignment is critical for all who minister with a kingdom calling, especially for intercessors in our profession.]

How do you know when you are ready to step out? Well, after you read this book, you may want to take a certification class, or you may want to just start out on your own (and WISE can help you with that too).

So again, how do you know you are ready? You may have the finances, the training, and even the potential clients in your area, but how do you know that you won't be beaten up in the spirit? When the seven sons of Sceva (Acts 19:13-16) were casting out evil spirits, one spirit said something very interesting: "Jesus I know, and Paul I know about, but who are you?" This was directly before they beat up the sons and tore off their clothes. The enemy knew the authority of Paul and of Jesus, but these sons of Sceva were not proven in spiritual warfare, nor in having knowledge of the Lord.

Is your name known in hell? Is your authority proven?

Is your ministry known in the prophetic, in intercession, in deliverance?

What do you have to work with?

You need to be able to assess your strengths and weaknesses as an intercessor.

What gifts do you possess? What are your strengths? Also, WISE staff can advise and assist you by guiding you through some of our master offerings. Can you minister to your clients successfully by yourself or do you need to be a part of a team so that your clients get effective ministry?

Are you more apostolic or prophetic; can you prophesy? This is not an absolute requirement, but is very helpful. Are you willing to learn?

Are you filled with the Spirit with the evidence of speaking in tongues? Asked another way, do you have a prayer language?

As I mentioned earlier in this book, the baptism in Holy Spirit is the gateway into the supernatural. This is where you operate as an intercessor. Paul asked in Acts 19:1-2

> "While Apollos was at Corinth, Paul took the road through the interior and arrived at Ephesus. There he found some disciples and asked them, 'Did you receive Holy Spirit when you believed?' They answered, 'No, we have not even heard that there is a Holy Spirit.'"

(This is a subsequent and preferably coincident experience. Ideally, right after someone is saved he can be filled with Holy Spirit, but in my case, I received the baptism a number of months later.)

These and other questions need to be answered. Ask the Lord if you are ready. If you do not feel ready, or if you do not have a peace, then wait and continue to learn. Go over this material again, but do not be afraid of the enemy's retaliation if you proceed. The enemy can smell fear is attracted by it.

Fear will be the greatest obstacle for you and any other believer to overcome. It is the opposite of faith. Fear will test your faith; conversely, you fight fear with your faith. Remember, "God has allotted to each a measure of faith" (Rom. 12:3 NASB). This is the measure you will need in order to function and do what God has called you to do. You already have the faith, just learn to apply it and, like Peter, walk on the water to Jesus, who is calling you.

Personal Testimony — Not Being Ready

A personal testimony of when I was not ready: When Liz was pregnant with Nathanael, I was heaven-bent on starting a church out of our home. We were not attending church and I had no covering. We had a handful of people to whom I was preaching and ministering, but we experienced oppression and spiritual warfare at a level I was not used to. I was dealing with the territorial spirits in the Tampa Bay area and was not ready for that warfare. My supervisor had just told me that we were going to rewrite the system that I had just spent eighteen months writing (as a computer programmer). Then Liz gave birth to Nathanael via a C-section, and I had to take care of my new son. I was depressed; the church was not working. In addition, I was not sleeping. I felt alone. I remember complaining to the Lord, "No one believes in me." Right away the Lord said, "I believe in you!" Jesus came to me and said that he would never leave me. It was a great trial. It was during that time I experienced the benefit of one-on-one counseling. However, the little church folded. This experience helped me realize the importance of being properly aligned.

What Is Spiritual Alignment?

Question: *Are you joined to and aligned with someone who has gone higher than you in God?*

Favor is transferable. Who walks in the favor of God and understands your calling, gifts, strengths, and weaknesses?

It is a *spiritual principle* that those who are aligned with or covered by an apostolic leader (very important) operate in the *same authority* of that leader. Put another way, those enemies who can be defeated by the apostolic leader can also be defeated by anyone aligned with that leader. Those enemies who come against anyone aligned with that leader also come against the leader himself, so the leader needs to know the people with whom he is aligning (or covering) fairly well, otherwise he may experience unnecessary spiritual warfare from people who are not properly aligned with God.

With whom are you aligned? Who is your apostle? Who can speak into your life, and who has gone further than you in the Spirit, not just in your specific calling as an intercessor? Who can break things off of you when you need it? Who knows your calling and gifting; who can bless and commission you? Be sure to have a person (or persons) you can trust in your life, someone whom you can bounce ideas off. It may be a coach—Paul had Barnabas.

Module 8: Endnotes

1. Transcribed from Elizabeth Alves and team leaders'. "Intercession Training." Intercessors International, 2005.

2. MacArthur, John. *Strange Fire: The Danger of Offending the Holy Spirit with Counterfeit Worship.* Nashville: Thomas Nelson, 2013.

Recommended Additional Resources for Readers and Students

Books

Vermaak, Natasha. *Repentance, Cleansing Your Generational Bloodline: Restoring the First Estate* (Vol. 1)

Hamon, Bill. *Apostles, Prophets, and the Coming Moves of God.*

Cook, Dr. Bruce. *Partnering with the Prophetic*

Website articles

Mike Parsons, "Gateways of the Spirit," www.freedomarc.wordpress.com/2013/11/26/gateways-of-the-spirit

DVDs/CDs/MP3s

Robert Henderson, "Operating in the Courts of Heaven" (Parts 1-4), www.roberthenderson.org.

Ian Clayton, "Supernatural Encounters 101" conference set. www.resources.sonofthunder.org

People

Dutch Sheets, Dutch Sheets Ministries | dutchsheets.org

STRATEGIC BREAKTHROUGH

The words were that God saw me as a knight in shining armor, and he was going to connect me with other significant people; I was going to have a turn of events and God was preparing a people for me to impart to and impact. That's the basis of the diagram, and I put it aside and went on with things, but at the same time Charles was saying to me multiple times to "hang in there until June; don't do anything drastic until June because something is going to happen in June."

What's happened is that your diagram was incredibly accurate! In retrospect it's amazing, and when I show it to people and give them the story behind it, the most common thing I hear is wow!

Here's what happened: We gathered all our forces and did a major effort to sell via our public seminars. To put this in perspective, three years ago we had approx. eight hundred people in these seminars, and this year the first six cities that we promoted in, which are cities where we have a good-standing client base, we had a total of one registration. It was clear that God was saying that it was time for this to be over. We couldn't have tried to do that badly! There was supernatural involvement in this. I saw this as the turn of events which you had drawn in your picture.

I began searching for something else to do, and asking God what he wanted me to do. I was led providentially to a group called "Truth at Work," which organizes Christian CEO round tables. We're now going to be doing a video webinar round table with Christian CEOs meeting on a monthly basis, helping them grow their businesses and develop spiritually. I am absolutely convinced that this is the fulfillment of the words that you wrote down about God preparing a significant people group for me to impart to and impact. So...this all happened in June! We're talking about working with CEOs of Christian businesses around the country, and maybe even around the world, in these webinars.

I'm just here thinking Wow! This is incredible!"

— Dave K., Comstock Park, MI

8

"He said, 'LORD, you are the God of our people. You are the God who is in heaven. You rule over all of the kingdoms of the nations. Your hands are strong and powerful. No one can fight against you and win.'... All of the kingdoms of the surrounding countries began to have respect for God. They had heard how the LORD had fought against Israel's enemies" (II Chronicles 20:6, 29 NIRV).

Strategic Intelligence to Take All Seven Mountains

WISE is developing strategic intelligence to take and integrate all seven mountains together. This will result in further enabling the kingdom of God in the earth.

Each Mountain Needs a Specific Strategy

The strategy to advance a campaign on the government mountain is totally different than the one needed to produce a Christian film on the arts & entertainment mountain. Intercessors will, likewise, see differences for each mountain in the type and severity of spiritual warfare to expect and in the strategy needed to win the battle for culture.

One size definitely does not fit all when it comes to the strategies forintercession, prayer, and breakthrough. There are some universal strategiesfor all mountains; notably the strategy of using Scripture, because God's Wordalways produces results.

Okay. *I admit,* I just told you one size does not fit all mountains for intercession, prayer, and breakthrough strategies, but then I *immediately changed course* to say that Scripture can be a starting point strategy to reclaim any mountain. Don't get distracted!

The specific strategies and thoughts for each of the seven mountains cannot be an exhaustive list; it is, in fact, constantly developing as I travel, meet new clients, and encounter new situations. I will tell you that Liz and I have been involved in all seven mountains, so our experience is ongoing.

Some general principles* may make what I say here resemble the lighthearted three-part sermon outline—"I'm gonna tell you what I'll tell you, then I'll tell you, then I'll tell you what I told you." I've already stressed at least twice how important it is, as an intercessor, to maintain an intimate walk with our Lord, and how he is the source to which you look for guidance for both you and your client. In addition, you will instruct your client how important these two spiritual disciplines are for him or her.

When believers obey the truths in God's word, and seek him for guidance and direction, even just one or a small group can make a major impact!

In the strategies chart that follows, you'll notice that these two principles apply as valid strategies for multiple mountains, so they are listed at the bottom of the chart rather than for an individual mountain.[†]

Johnny Enlow says that the forces of darkness are at the summit of each of the seven mountains.[‡]

> "Starting with Rosh Hashanah of 2015, a seismic shift will take place in the same way that the seven years of plenty ended in Egypt. If a great earthquake happens on that day, consider it the Lord's grace clearly signaling that earth-rattling changes are upon us. On this day, there will be a great unplugging of the systems of this world. The Lord will call for a famine on the foundations that are not sourced from His kingdom."
>
> — Johnny Enlow, *The Seven Mountain Mantle*

Johnny says we will see the systematic crumbling of the systems

---

* in the Change Agent stories by Os Hillman
† A robust source of strategies to use for each mountain is found in Os Hillman's book, Change Agent: Engaging Your Passion to Be the One Who Makes a Difference.
‡ See my friend Johnny Enlow's excellent book The Seven Mountain Prophecy and, for specific strategies for the mountains, see The Seven Mountain Mantle, also by J. Enlow.

of this world, and goes on to declare the need for the modern-day Josephs to arise with solutions to avert or lessen catastrophes. I see the times as being similar to those in Noah's day—God will depose the enemy's seven mountain leaders who are currently set up, and in their place set up his Josephs. It is a time for new beginnings.

Let us begin with how the seven mountains of culture are connected. The goal is to develop a strategy for each mountain or sphere that you may be operating in and give you a strategy to connect those spheres or mountains when appropriate.

Defining 7M Interconnections

Family is connected to all of the other mountains and is the foundation for everything because it is the most basic relational unit.

- Education and government are interconnected.
- Arts & entertainment and media are interconnected.
- Business and religion are interconnected—e.g., WISE.
- Business fuels all of the other mountains with finances.§

We can see the sevenfold Spirit of the Lord reflected in these connections and, interestingly, could view these connections in the design of a menorah, where the middle candlestick is foundational and the other six candles are connected into pairs by the curved lines of the menorah.

Isaiah 11:2 states: "The Spirit of the Lord (Adonai, in some translations) will rest on him—the Spirit of wisdom and of understanding, the Spirit of counsel and of might, the Spirit of the knowledge and fear of the Lord."

Family, connected to all the other mountains, is foundational, like the center of the candlestick, and it reflects the importance of love, as is the compassionate nature of the Lord reflected in the name Adonai. Wisdom and understanding could be seen as the connected mountains of business and religion; counsel and might could be seen as arts & entertainment and media (and could reflect the mighty power of media, with its control over "message"). The final pairing of knowledge and fear of the Lord could be seen as the connected mountains of education and government.

As you review these connections, what does Holy Spirit say to you?

§ See my friend Johnny Enlow's excellent book *The Seven Mountain Prophecy* and, for specific strategies for the mountains, see *The Seven Mountain Mantle*, also by J. Enlow.

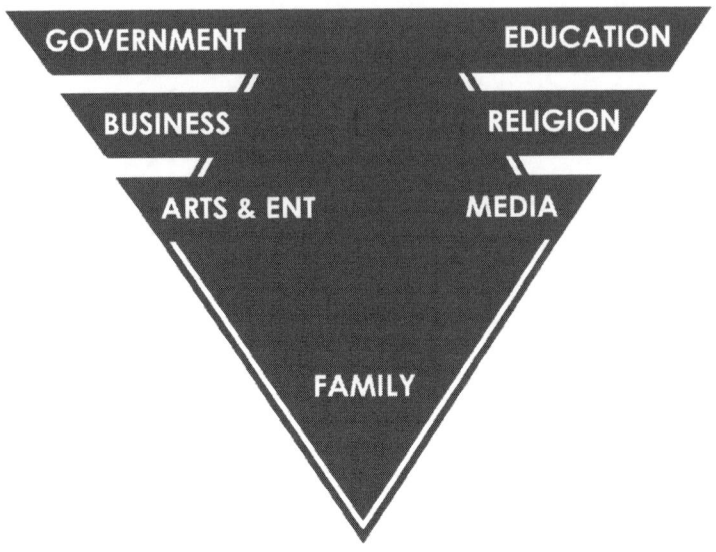

Figure 18 The Seven Mountain Menorah

The Coming Seven Moves of God in the Mountains

The Lord has been speaking to me about the seven thunders in Revelation being connected to the seven mountains. The seven thunders are seven moves of God, one move related to each of the mountains. The scroll on which this was written was sealed up for the end times and then eaten by John; it was sweet to his mouth, but bitter to his stomach (see Rev. 10:9).

> Then I saw another mighty angel coming down from heaven. He was robed in a cloud, with a rainbow above his head; his face was like the sun, and his legs were like fiery pillars. He was holding a little scroll, which lay open in his hand. He planted his right foot on the sea and his left foot on the land, and he gave a loud shout like the roar of a lion. When he shouted, the voices of the seven thunders spoke. And when the seven thunders spoke, I was about to write; but I heard a voice from heaven say, "Seal up what the seven thunders have said and do not write it down." … But in the days when the seventh angel is about to sound his trumpet, the mystery of God will be accomplished, just as he announced to his servants the prophets (Rev .10:1-4,7).

We are now in the days when the seventh angel is about to sound his trumpet! "Then the voice that I had heard from heaven spoke to me once more: 'Go, take the scroll that lies open in the hand of the angel who is standing on the sea and on the land'" (Rev. 10:8). The angel was standing on the sea (indicating humanity) and the land (indicating the marketplace). This is a move to *connect* the people to the marketplace and to *complete* the final work of God.

> So I went to the angel and asked him to give me the little scroll. He said to me, "Take it and eat it. It will turn your stomach sour, but 'in your mouth it will be as sweet as honey.'" I took the little scroll from the angel's hand and ate it. It tasted as sweet as honey in my mouth, but when I had eaten it, my stomach turned sour. Then I was told, "You must prophesy again about many peoples, nations, languages and kings" (Rev. 10:9-11).

Notice there is a *last days prophetic movement* coming which is related to the voice of the seven thunders, the content of which was *sealed up.*

The message of God in our day will be sweet (because we are speaking the exhilarating and fresh words of the Lord to each mountain) but in the outworking of it, the *digesting* of it, if you will, we—as God's Josephs—will have to endure the many shakings that are coming upon the world (but we will be victorious).

As the message continues in Revelation 10:11, "You must prophesy again about many peoples, nations, languages and kings." Notice many peoples (out of the sea), nations (sheep nations), languages and *kings* (indicating the marketplace). These seven end-time messages will be sent to *the entire earth* and to *all seven mountains of influence.*

Finally, John was given a reed and told to measure the temple (the religion mountain) (see Rev. 11:1). The implication is that this event was next in the sequence, *but it may not be.* My opinion is that it is next in the sequence of chronological events. The religion mountain is very important to God.

The book of Revelation next mentions the two witnesses. Their power is to defy death and to exact the wrath of God on the earth during the great tribulation, but there must be a move of God in each mountain beforehand! Maybe God will use *you* to prophesy and release one or more of these seven thundering voices, which are seven moves of God—one for each sphere or mountain of influence. Like John I say, "Even so, come quickly, Lord Jesus!"

The Tipping Point and Tipping Point Conferences

Since 2000, Lance Wallnau[¶] and Os Hillman[**] have given many talks about the marketplace ministry strategy for taking the seven mountains in US culture (and have been talking about it more since 2009). Christians who desire to reform our culture have changed their strategy in order to honor the tipping point. Early on, the strategy focused on placing Christians at high points—points of leadership (affluence and/or influence)—in the seven mountains. A weakness of that strategy was that it could be a slow process (and often quite expensive) to place only a few leaders in high places. We noticed that the morality of a company (or segment of society, such as a city agency) could not be dictated downward to those working at lower positions.

Another aspect of societal change offers more promise for easier, and perhaps faster, results—the aspect of a tipping point. Missionaries have observed this phenomenon.

Although it takes only a small percentage (4 percent) of leaders to create an appreciable influence on a segment of society, it doesn't take much more of the grassroots population (a little over 10 percent) to influence one.

Currently, those Christians who desire to reform all seven segments (mountains) of society are shifting their foci to concentrate on creating tipping points. They are focused now on making more disciples at the grass roots level on each mountain rather than placing a few Christians in high areas of affluence and influence. The result can be to, essentially, tip the mountain over through the influence of that critical percentage of Christians exerting their grass roots influence (enhanced by the spiritual power of our Creator).

What does 7-UP have to do with a tipping point? Well, picture in your mind the seven mountains of culture (business, education, media, etc.) tipped over so that the playing field of each mountain (the base) is now at the top, and a base of Christians have access to

---

¶ You can find more info on Lance Wallnau at www.lancelearning.biz.
** You can find more info on Os Hillman at www.marketplaceleaders.org.

the mountain peak, not just the top influencers. We are turning things upside-down (right-side up), hence the term "7-UP."

How can a PLI interact with that strategy? As you work with a business owner, you do not need to overlook possible clients and focus only on the most affluent and influential businesses; God can use any business as a change agent to help reform society. For instance, as you mentor your client on godly time management, the client places his first priority on quality time spent with God (which helps bring the insight and blessings God has intended from the religion mountain for the owner and his business, and empowers your intercession). As the client places his second priority on time spent with his spouse, and his third priority on time spent with his children, he honors God in a way that creates ripples of blessing in the family mountain. As the owner continues to align his priorities with God's priorities, he puts his (or her) business at the next (fourth) area of priority, which is in the proper position to receive the tangible and spiritual business mountain blessings God ordains for his business. Your intercession increases the spiritual power at work in this process.

The Tipping Point We See Now in Our Culture

What is a tipping point? A critical juncture, a defining moment in a series of events (think economic, cultural, social, etc.,) at which time a sequence of significant, and often momentous and irreversible, reactions occur. We are at many tipping points in society: governmental, financial, economic, spiritual, etc. These critical times call for a gathering—even a solemn assembly—of God's *emerging Josephs and Daniels.* Will you join us? You were created to be a world changer and history maker. Will you be one of the delegates from your state or nation? God will make his voice and will known to you. Will you make your voice known to the other world changers present? *You are needed.*

WISE Ministries' Tipping Point Mission

WISE Ministries International is assembling marketplace and ministerial leaders like you in all seven spheres of influence,—modern-day Josephs and Daniels who will overcome worldly mindsets and economic systems and their limitations with heavenly perspectives. Based upon the book *Tipping Point* by Malcolm Gladwell,[1] the Tipping Point conferences and networking meetings sponsored by WISE)†† touch on how small changes can turn into much larger ones. That pretty much describes a lot of the facets of our lives today. You can't even watch *Fox News* without seeing several tipping points, most of which are being ignored by the "experts" in government or business. There are tipping points all around us that people are unaware of. Like the proverbial frog who sits in a pot of water that is beginning to boil, they are not even aware that they are slowly being boiled to death.

> *WISE, the major Tipping Point sponsor, has an anointing for favor and breakthrough, a spiritual ability like that of an ice-breaking ship that breaks open paths of access and supply lines of provision that have been frozen within the cold, dark waters of this Babylonian world system.*

Ongoing Tipping Point Events Sponsored by WISE

The Lord is raising up modern-day Josephs and Daniels and those like the sons of Issachar who "knew what the times demanded" (I Chron. 12:32). We believe that God's angels and anointing will be available to strengthen and empower you to finish the race that is before you. Join us at Tipping Point events.‡‡

Goals for Tipping Point Conferences and Network Meetings:

Fine-tune yourself (and thus, your ability to help your clients) to be ready to hear God's voice for your life and your city.

Help your clients, and yourself, get up to speed on topics and issues that affect your everyday life and the safety and well-being of your family and employees.

Receive a new coat of many colors in the presence of people of many colors.

Build relationships and alliances for the purpose of bringing

---

†† Find one near you at coachmybusiness.com.

‡‡ Go to www.TippingPointGathering.com for information and to register for our regional/national gatherings. Visit www.TippingPointNW.com for information and to register for our monthly dinner gatherings in cities across the nation.

kingdom solutions to your location.

Order your clients' (and your) steps for convergence so they (and you) will not waste time and will be in the right place at the right time.

Receive spiritual strategies for success in your and your clients' mountain(s) of influence.

Receive personal spiritual ministry from the WISE ministry team, which will provide direction and confirmation to open your spiritual senses, and give understanding of the times and seasons in which we live.

God can show you the technology, healing, demographic, and spiritual waves that are coming and how to respond to them to get his people ready. He is going to show you the new economic super cycles that are coming, the new trends, and new inventions.

A major blessing a PLI can be to the business community is in his ability to help each owner transform his enterprise into a kingdom company. As a professional level intercessor, you can partner with your clients to create kingdom companies and bring a company everything it needs to function in its destiny. You are one of the Josephs and Daniels of the twenty-first century.

Now you have the opportunity to be "trained up in the way you should go" and have a career that can serve and change the nations. Will you answer the call?

Module 9: Endnotes

1. Gladwell, Malcolm. *The Tipping Point: How Little Things Can Make a Big Difference.* New York: Back Bay Books, 2002.

Recommended Additional Resources for Readers/Students

Books

Hillman, Os. *Change Agent: Engaging Your Passion to Be the One Who Makes a Difference* [which contains a chapter for reclaiming each of the seven mountains, and relates stories of successful culture change, often by a single change agent or small group, and the strategies used to accomplish those successes].

Enlow, Johnny. *The Seven Mountain Mantle*

Ferguson, David. *Top 10 Intimacy Needs* (Intimacy Monograph Series)

Femrite, Tommi. *Invading the Seven Mountains With Intercession: How to Reclaim Society Through Prayer*

Wallnau, Lance, and Bill Johnson. *Invading Babylon: The 7 Mountain Mandate*

Cook, Dr. Bruce. *Partnering With The Prophetic: Portfolios, Protocols, Patterns & Processes*

DVDs/CDs/MP3s

Os Hillman. "Reclaiming the 7 Mountains of Culture Introduction." DVD. www.tgifbookstore.com.

Lance Wallnau. "The 7 Mountain Mandate: Impacting Culture Discipling Nations." DVD. www.morningstarministries.org.

Os Hillman, Lance Wallnau, Johnny Enlow, and others. "7 Mountain Strategies: Keys for Cultural Influence." Audio CD Series. www. tgifbookstore.com

Website articles

Os Hillman, TGIF Daily Marketplace Devotional, www.marketplaceleaders.org/tgif

Videos

www.TippingPoint.TV

People

Os Hillman, Marketplace Leaders
www.marketplaceleaders.org
and his TGIF bookstore www.tgifbookstore.com

YOUR CHOICES

"I have been blessed with WISE Marketplace Ministries. I have enjoyed our prayer times, meetings, and prophetic words. I also have been blessed by the intercessor who was assigned to us and the details of her prayer times, which she e-mailed to us. This has blessed me to see the type of prayer going on behind the scenes. May God richly bless WISE and open new doors to new businesses."

— Daniel G., Austin, TX

"Charles and Liz have played a major intercessory role in my personal journey. In this end-time season, it is absolutely critical that the arrows of intercession we shoot hit the mark all the time."

— Patrick Kuwana
Founder, Crossover Transformation Group
Johannesburg, South Africa

9

WISE Ministries International

WISE is a pioneer in the new "strategic intelligence"space, otherwise called "coaching and intercession for enterprises." Dr. Charles and Liz Robinson founded WISE Ministries International in 2005 tobe a training, equipping, and service ministry to businesses, ministries, and enterprises in all seven mountains of culture. WISE provides intercession, kingdom consulting, and timely prophetic words in all seven of the spheres of culture, sometimes referred to as the seven mountains of culture: business, government, arts & entertainment, media, education, family, and religion.

WISE services provide a vibrant training, consulting, and healing ministry for developing and equipping the body of Christ to live in victory through experiencing the delivering power of Jesus Christ, our Lord and Savior. WISE teaches people how to incorporate prayer into their enterprises, and trains and imparts into the next generation.

WISE is active in:

Government - by supporting local and national candidates, by impacting the governmental mountain through DC-based intercessory teams, and through its Gates2DC.com ministry;

Arts & Entertainment - through the Gates2Hollywood.com ministry and association with several major Christian film studios and releases;

Family - through its marriage counseling ministry;

Education - through its ministry at foundational universities, such as Harvard University;

Business - through entrance, via intercession and/or coaching, into over one hundred companies in numerous industries;

Religion - through support of church and parachurch ministries;

Media - via Internet; via satellite—the On The Way Network and the Cross Network, which covers the globe, with access to over 120 million people.

WISE employs intercessors and coaches all over the world in a decentralized model, utilizing the latest in Internet technologies, to teach people how to incorporate prayer into their enterprises.

WISE maintains offices in Hollywood, California; Austin, Texas; and Washington, D.C.; and we can also travel to enterprises for on-site initial consultations, assessments, and evaluations.

Do you want your intercession business to be a part of the WISE network? If so, there are three options available for you, which are described below and summarized in a table following this text. It is your decision.

Option 1: WISE Certifies You and Refers Clients to You

You attend our certification class, either in person or online, and sign our nondisclosure agreement when you receive your course material (since in your class you will receive many forms which are the intellectual property of WISE).

We work together. You can utilize our front-end (initial consult) process, our back office (invoicing and accounts receivable), receive referrals from us, know exactly how we charge, be able to offer your clients all of our master offerings, etc., and have my *ongoing* mentoring (even after you are certified as an intercessor).

There is no charge for this other than the charge for the certification class. We both make money on an ongoing basis. You represent WISE; we refer clients to you (based upon availability), you refer clients to us, and you are their intercessor. (WISE staff will review the compensation plan with you.)

This option means that, in regards to intercession, you will become a part of WISE and will not be doing your own thing. You need to think about this. With the CPI certification curriculum, I teach you how to do what we do. There are numerous proprietary details at this stage of the course to learn from.

Option 1 is the closest possible connection to WISE you can have.

Remember, there is no charge to be a WISE CPI, but if you prefer to run an independent intercession service, you'll want to choose option 2. With option 1, as a WISE CPI, you will also sign a two-year non-compete agreement, which basically means that you agree, upon separation from WISE, to not compete directly with us for a duration of two years (when and even *if* that happens; hopefully we will be working together until the rapture or the second coming, depending on your eschatology!).

Option 2: WISE Certifies You as a CPI and Licenses You as an Independent PLI

You attend our certification class, either in person or online, and sign our nondisclosure agreement when you receive your course material (since in the class you will receive many forms which are the intellectual property of WISE).

You do the work, benefit from your connection with us, and conform to the standards required in bearing the WISE name. I license you to do what we do. (You do not need to bear our name if you want to have your own name, but there is value and name recognition with our name, which has been building since 2005.)

With option 2, you become a certified CPI and will be connected to WISE, but your business will be independent of WISE. Being a certified and licensed WISE intercessor, you get to use the WISE name and logo—everything—or your own, whichever you prefer. You become an extension of us, yet build your business independently, keep all the money, and have access to all of our methods, processes, and procedures on an ongoing basis. When we receive a breakthrough technique, strategy, etc., you receive it too, because you are a part of WISE.

Picture it as similar to your starting a McDonald's, except you are purchasing a WISE license rather than a McDonald's franchise.

This option requires an up-front cost, and an annual fee (after the first year) for ongoing support, which includes a two-day onsite visit for one-on-one training in marketing, e-mail marketing, website setup and design—everything you need to get you started on the fast track

Think of this license option as going into business for yourself but not by yourself. With the CPI certification, I teach you how to do what we do [but option 1 helps you go to a greater depth than with option

Options Summary for PLI's Connections to WISE			
Detail	**Option 1**	**Option 2**	**Option 3**
	Certified PLI, working with WISE	*Certified, Independent, Licensed PLI*	*Independent, not certified PLI*
May use WISE's IP?	Yes	Yes	No
Sign Nondisclosure?	Yes, because of IP	Yes, because of IP	No
Sign Noncompete?	Yes	No, because of license	No, because has no IP
Cost	Course (Note: salary after course is paid by WISE)	Course, license, annual fee for services	Cost of published book
Who pays you?	WISE	Your client through your business	Your client through your business
Your client is...	WISE client with you as PLI	Your client through your business	Your client through your business
May use WISE's front-end?	Yes	No	No
Includes WISE's back office?	Yes	No	No
May use the WISE name?	Yes	Yes, if you choose to No, if not	No
Conforms to WISE standards?	Yes	Yes, if you choose to use WISE name No, if not	No
Gets referrals from WISE?	Yes	No	No
Ongoing WISE mentoring available?	Yes	Some ongoing support Comes with annual fee	No
IAMIN membership?	Free for 1 year	Free for 1 year	Available for a fee
IAMIN referrals?	Yes, for 1 year, more if renew membership	Yes, for 1 year, more if renew membership	Available if you join IAMIN

Figure 5 Options Summary for PLI's Connections to WISE

2. Remember, there is no charge to be a WISE CPI, but it is exclusive of your doing your own independent intercession and business administration (option 2)].

Option 3: You Read the Text Only and Are an Independent PLI

You do the work. You read the book (which is based on the certification course manual, and contains a subset of the material in the course manual). You do not receive the forms that are the intellectual property of WISE. You do not sign a nondisclosure agreement. With this subset of what we do, you can run your own intercession business *independently of WISE.* You can contact WISE if you wish to purchase consulting services about questions you might have, such as how much to charge.

Note that with options 1 and 2, I teach about the PLI profession and pepper it with some of the processes, forms, and procedures that we use at WISE so you can be successful on your own, and there is much more: I can also train you in the WISE way so that you can work with us.

You can be connected with WISE in greater depth by being a WISE CPI (option 1) or going through certification as a CPI, purchasing a license, and maintaining an ongoing connection with our methods, processes, and procedures (option 2).

The bottom line for option 3 is this: I won't give everything away if you are going to do your own thing and compete with us using our own methods.

It's decision time! [The chart on the left summarizes the benefits/restrictions of options 1–3 for a PLI's relationship with WISE.]

Licensing and Commissioning Leaders in the Marketplace

As a part of our commissioning, we (WISE) license and commission (we formerly used the word ordain) leaders in the marketplace. WISE recognizes that God has called leaders in all the seven mountains, not just in the religious mountain. Accordingly, WISE recognizes that these ministers do not differ to God in importance as compared to those who hold traditional ministry positions in church, or who are supported by the church, such as missionaries. WISE further recognizes that those who have the ministry gift of apostle, prophet, pastor, etc. can function in their spheres of influence, i.e., in one or more of the seven mountains. WISE recognizes how vital it is, as a person progresses in his spiritual calling, to have a person or a group honor him and acknowledge his authority and sphere of influence by setting him in, or consecrating him, and being there as a guiding hand. If you or a leader you know could benefit from licensing (which is akin to a dating period for one year) or from commissioning, please contact our office to receive a list of requirements and benefits.

Confidentiality and Intellectual Property (IP)

We have been developing these offerings since 2005, and have touched thousands of people with this ministry. We know what we are doing. You can make a part-time or full-time income if you work with us, but please keep our processes, procedures, and intellectual property confidential. We require the two-year non-compete agreement so that if/when you separate from us you do not directly compete with us. It is better to work with us, as we can funnel work opportunities your way and handle the details so that you can grow your business, based on your preference of coaching and/or intercession. We provide a strong reputation in the industry, and are a spokesperson for it. In fact, we are one of its pioneers, continually shaping the industries of professional level intercession and spiritual, life, and executive coaching.

Certification Courses

WISE currently offers four certification courses in a series called "Let Heaven Invade the Seven Mountains of Culture."

Volume 1: *WISE 7M Intercessor Certification Guide*

Other Planned Volumes

Volume 2: WISE 7M Leadership Implementation Guide will inform CEOs and business leaders how to identify, engage, manage, and release intercessors, corporate pastors, spiritual coaches, and chief revelatory officers into their organizations for their corporate and personal wellbeing.*

Volume 3: WISE 7M Coaches Certification Guide (spiritual coach, life coach, executive coach, and executive leadership coach options).[†]

Volume 4: WISE 7M Generals Level Certification Guide is for the top marketplace leaders in all seven mountains who need the best in "spiritual survival" training (for dealing with all kinds of spiritual dilemmas). Leaders learn how to deal with (take authority over and get to the root of) many situations which can arise in their global enterprises.[‡]

Course Schedule and Format Options

Certification courses happen monthly. Check

- markteplaceintercessors.com,
- marketplaceceos,
- marketplacecoaches.com, and/or
- marketplacegenerals.com for prices and offering dates.

All four of the courses listed above are available in two formats:

- *Group and Fast Track:* Two-and-a-half days of live on-site training
- *Independent Study:* All modules are divided over twelve weeks.

Both formats offer the student impartation, wisdom, and experience from personal contact with WISE instructors.

---

* See marketplaceCEOS.com for more information.
† See marketplacecoaches.com for more information.
‡ See marketplacecoaches.com for more information.

Why Certify as a CPI (Certified Professional Intercessor)?

Reading this book without participating in a live class or recorded sessions will prove to be valuable; however, if you wish to receive certification and full impartation (including proprietary material, sample forms and processes, etc.), you will need to attend the classes, or at least view the recorded version of the classes and complete the exercises.

Certification offers you the following benefits:

- Opportunity for you to enter the exciting new career field of Professional Level Intercession with the designation CPI. To obtain certification from WISE Ministries as a Certified Professional Intercessor (CPI) and to be able to use that designation after your name, you will need to attend the two-and-a-half day training, either on location or via the videos/webinars. In other words, we want to meet you and work with you personally in order to certify you.
- Full access to proprietary material, sample forms, and processes which are available to only those who attend the 7M Intercessor Certification Course
- Opportunity for you to work for WISE or to stay independent
- Opportunity for you to receive referrals from WISE and IAMIN (see below)
- Opportunity to participate in our national network
- Membership for one year in IAMIN—The International ApostolicMarketplace Intercessors Network[§]
- Interface with the International Association of Marketplace Coaches (IAMC)[¶]

[§] See marketplaceintercessors.com, and iamcert.com for more information.
[¶] See marketplacecoaches.com for more detail.

Vision for IAMIN

To unify and certify professional intercessors for marketplace ministry in a seven mountains framework; to uphold certain standards of excellence and codes of conduct in marketplace ministry; to be a shining example of integrity in kingdom business and ministry to the world; to be a standard that people can relate to.

Our Five-Fold Purpose

1. Fellowship
2. Education
3. Ethical standards of excellence through membership and certification
4. Accountability
5. Unification

The Benefits of Membership

- Ongoing education in intercessory methods
- Discounted certification tracks for additional courses, such as kingdom consulting and "sons of Issachar" training
- Preferential intercessory opportunities
- May attend yearly conferences
- Opportunity to fellowship with like-gifted peers
- Apostolic oversight
- Become part of a worldwide network, a new wineskin
- An opportunity to be a licensed and/or ordained marketplace intercessor
- Opportunity for relationship-based accountability
- Membership certificate and card
- Leadership that has almost a decade's experience of supporting and interceding for over one hundred companies, and growing

Requirements for Membership to IAMIN:

Love the Lord Jesus Christ; have been saved for at least one year.

Have ministry/some prophetic experience and have been a counselor or deliverance minister.

Possess familiarity with a computer, a word processor, and typing skills.

Have access to an Internet connection.

The emphasized sentence is not required for membership, it is required for success.

ABOUT THE AUTHOR

Dr. Charles and Liz Robinson have pioneered a global breakthrough in marketplace ministry through WISE Ministries International—a ministry that empowers leaders by providing a combination of business, spiritual, and prophetic support—using their impressive history of degrees and experience as a foundational guide. Both ordained ministers with the CIAN, and as current directors of the IAMIN, Charles and Liz maintain offices in Austin, Hollywood, and Washington, D.C. in order to personally minister on the mountains of business, entertainment, and government.

Charles is also the convener of the bi-annual Tipping Point Gathering 7-UP Unconference—an interactive three-day meeting of key leaders from the seven mountains of influence.

MORE FROM WISE MINISTRIES

WISE Prayer Request Website and Theme song

WISE Prayer request site and theme song:
www.coachmybusiness.com/prayer-request.php

WISE Online Store Links for DVDs

DVDs from WISE (provided to Certification Course Students):

Intercession **2.0** http://fur.ly/ao8i

Taking **Company to Next Level Spiritually**
http://fur.ly/ao8if

Opening **Global Gates of Access and Provision**
http://fur.ly/ao8ig

Tipping **Point Media from WISE online store**
Tipping Point 2013 Gathering Conference DVD (also available on CD and MP3) http://fur.ly/ao8h

Our iPhone/Android Mobile App

As you move forward with your career as a PLI, use our WISE app to submit your prayer requests, read our blog, find out where our next gatherings are going to be, or receive a prophetic word. Also, as the Lord leads, advise your clients to use our app.

Figure 21 Graphic for WISE App

WISE Ministries International websites

Main prayer websites:
prayformybusiness.com
prayformyministry.com

Intercessor certification:
IAMCERT.com
marketplaceintercessors.com

Our 7M sites:
tippingpointgathering.com
7mcouncil.com
charlesrobinson.com

Our coaching sites:
coach4mylife.com
marketplacecoaches.com
coachmybusiness.com[2]

WISE provides monthly newsletters in "The Joseph Blog," available at:

coachmybusiness.com/marketplaceministry

The 7M book series is available at the site:

www.letheaveninvade7m.com

For information and to register for monthly gatherings, visit:

www.tippingpointnw.com

Site to purchase *Let Heaven Invade the Seven Mountains of Culture*:

www.letheaveninvade7m.com

9676276R00073

Printed in Great Britain
by Amazon.co.uk, Ltd.,
Marston Gate.